T0095862

Tanks
for the Memories

Floatation Tank Talks

by
Dr. John C. Lilly
and E.J. Gold

Tanks

for the Memories:

Floatation Tank Talks

Previously unpublished transcripts of talks of
Dr. John C. Lilly and E.J. Gold.

with an introduction by
Lee Perry
Edited by Lee Perry and Faustin Bray

Gateways/ IDHHB, Inc.
Publishers

Copyright 1995 by Gateways
All Rights Reserved. Printed in the U.S.A.
First Printing.

Cover Art
A Wee Slip Of A Girl, Oil on Canvas, 60" x 96", E.J. Gold.

Cover Design by Nancy Christie

Illustrations by E.J. Gold

No part of this publication may be reproduced or transmitted in any form or by any means, electronic or mechanical, including photocopy, recording, or any information storage and retrieval system now known or to be invented, without permission in writing from the copyright holder, except by a reviewer who wishes to quote brief passages in connection with a review written for inclusion in a magazine, newspaper or broadcast.

The first chapter was delivered as a lecture at California Institute of Technology, Pasadena, CA. Chapters two and three appeared previously under the title, *John Lilly on Floatation Tanks* compiled by Faustin Bray, 1989, *Floating* magazine. E.J. Gold's talks were published on audio tape as *Tank Talks* by Union Label Recordings.

Library of Congress Cataloging-in-Publication Data
Lilly, John Cunningham, 1915-
     Tanks for the memories: floatation tank talks/ by John C. Lilly and E.J. Gold.
        p. cm.
    ISBN: 0-89556-071-2 (trade paper: alk. paper)
     1. Sensory deprivation--Therapeutic use. 2. Altered states of consciousness.3. Consciousness. I. Gold, E.J. II. Title.
RC489.S44L544 1995
154.4--dc20
                                    95-38869
                                       CIP

Table of Contents

Introduction

I'm not sure what possessed me that day when I swerved sharply and ended up here. I always thought I was different, a black sheep, but didn't want anyone else to know it. I did the things I thought everyone else did, such as go to school, rollerskate in Bronx Park, look at the pictures in museums, read all the fairy tales and mystery stories in the public library, laugh uncontrollably at the wrong times when I didn't want to be seen or heard laughing. I worked in the Joubert Cie perfume factory screwing tops on bottles quickly with both hands at the same time, walked the streets of Manhattan from river to river to see what was on them, played volleyball at Camp Nature Friends, listened to music at the Apollo Theatre and Birdland, studied modern dance with Jacqueline Hairston, the most beautiful woman in the universe, folk danced every Friday night, thought I was too fat, too young, too different, too quiet, too smart, too stupid, protested the loss of civil rights, got married, moved to Cleveland, had kids, moved to Los Angeles, Israel, back to Los Angeles, and got a teaching credential.

My second year of teaching I had a job 15 minutes from my Los Angeles house, across Elysian Park in the Mexican American barrio, Lincoln Heights. I was assigned to a third grade classroom and I was getting everything up and running, the school was buzzing with the new semester, and there was a most unhappy teacher at Albion St. School who obviously would not make it through the year. In fact she looked as if she wouldn't make it through the hour. She told me that she taught "Special Education" and she couldn't cope, she couldn't handle it, and wouldn't somebody please do something to help.

I am a sucker for helping others. I've done this same thing more times than I care to tell where I'm listening to someone's sad story and before I remember what I am doing, I volunteer for a job that I am sorry about very soon. I liked the idea of getting out of the mainstream and being free to experiment in my new classroom. I was told that one of my most important jobs was to keep the kids in my new class out of the office. Many of these children had severe behavior problems and the office was used as the last disciplinary resort. There were 18 children in the class between the ages of nine and thirteen. They had to score below "normal" on an IQ test to get into that classroom. There were sixteen boys and two girls, fourteen blacks and four Chicanos. Three kids walked to school and the rest came by bus. They came from the low income housing project downtown and had been out on their own earning some form of a living for years. Waiting for the school bus in the morning, they were the audience for the fights, the scandals, the knifings and threats of knifings that are or were the life of the projects. I thought I was tough until I heard these kids download at the morning "Show and Tell."

They let me know very quickly that they would do regular "school" stuff for 10 minutes at most, and then there would be an assortment of behaviors that signalled me to watch out, I was about to get in trouble. Leonard, our shorty, would sit glassy-eyed, staring at Jupiter (or Mars), tapping his pencil. Tyrone hated the sound of the pencil tapping and began to strategize pencil tap stopping.

Johnny would slump over on the desk, head on its side, arms dangling, making a sound between a moan and a gasp which seemed to mean he had just suffered badly from over-work and was seeing if he could ever recover.

Ricardo paced. He paced as if he was about to go somewhere, but then he would pause, look down at the floor, shake his head side to side and turn around walking in another direction. James was very sensitive to the air currents, and when Ricardo passed his desk several times, you could see him tighten ready to pounce on the one who was disturbing his environment. The environmental balance in the classroom was very delicate.

Their style of conflict resolution was to approach each other very slowly, shoulders back, elbows straight, hands in fists, leading with the chest, eyes maintaining a glaring contact. When the bodies were almost touching, the vibration began, "mmmmm. . ." . This was the threat of, the warning that "mother-----r" was to be invoked. Survival of the slickest triumphed.

The classroom was on the first floor of a very old Victorian building; it was the oldest classroom building in

Los Angeles, with tall, narrow windows and low window sills. The biggest boys would always maneuver their prey towards the windows—I thought it was to increase the threat to the opponent—but it was probably aimed at increasing how I perceived the threat, since the thought of one of the kids being thrown out of a window seemed to make me crazy. I was able to be moved from acting like a constant, rational, dependable guide to acting as an irrational, predictable, authority figure, guaranteed to get everyone in trouble.

And then there was big Helen, always right, always fair, and always maligned, with her big voice that would just boom, bringing anything and everything to a state of vibrational calamity. I was tough, raised in New York City and at home on the streets, but this scenario was beyond my imagination. It was beyond what Hollywood imagined 5 years later when *Blackboard Jungle* showed how bad the schools had become. I did not know what to do. Every day I went home and cried. There just didn't seem to be anything else to do.

After 2 weeks of tears I decided that there must be a reason that a situation as bad as this one could exist. The reason I came up with was that these kids made so much trouble in school because they couldn't learn. They had obviously failed at school because it was necessary to fail at school to get into my classroom. If I could help them to learn, they would be able to do fine at school. I wanted to show them how to learn and in order to do that I had to find out how I learned and that became my quest. How do I learn?

I assembled information on learning and it seemed that everything was related to learning so I considered everything. At that time Vance Norum, a bio-energetics therapist and friend contacted me. He was writing a Master's Thesis on the Isolation Tank and its effect on psychological test scores and was looking for subjects. I had never heard of the isolation tank, but he described it as completely dark and quiet with all the things that clamor for attention removed, so I thought this was exactly the right place to study the learning process. I volunteered as a subject and that was how I got to spend my first hour floating in a tank.

The tank was in a garage on a very ordinary, tract-house lined street in Mar Vista, California I didn't realize that I was scared until I got there. After an orientation and a shower, I climbed up two steps, raised the lid at the top of the wooden box, and lowered myself into a saline solution. I lay down on my back and the first thing I noticed was the sensation of popping up to the surface of the water. I have never been able to float in a pool. Only my head stays out of the water while my body sinks. Here, I was like a cork, with my face, chest and knees out of the water. I never felt anything like that before and I liked it. I also was never in such complete darkness before except maybe in a dream. It was really dark. My fear became huge mushroom stems growing out of my back and anchoring me to the floor of the tank. While I was in the tank and when I got out, I could see things or understand or notice, I wasn't even sure, I just knew that something happened floating around in that tank that had never happened to me before, and since I was on a learning quest, this was obviously a very important part of my quest.

Glenn Perry was the tank maker and I met him at a party in his house. I was surprised the next day when he called and said something pretty close to: "I'm scared of you. Will you go out with me?" "Whoa, pay attention" went this voice inside of me and I said something pretty close to: "That sounds like an offer I can't refuse. Yes." It took a very short time for us to become a couple and want to be together a lot of the time, and we needed to find a way to make that happen. My teaching was now working; the kids liked coming to school and I thought I had done something useful with my seven teaching years. Glenn and I began the business of making and selling isolation tanks, Samadhi Tanks. We never had any business experience, but lack of experience had never stopped either one of us before so Glenn quit his computer job while I finished the rest of the school year before jumping into the abyss.

This was the turning point. I was now joined to others in a new universe without physical boundaries, but connected by Dr. Lilly's work, especially his work with the Isolation Tank. All my connections and associations until that time seemed to flow along as a "reasonable," or recognizable path. School, marriage, politics, kids, teaching, homeowning, painting, dancing . . . isolation tank. It just didn't complete the picture. At that time I thought I understood what "the picture" did or could or should look like.

I grew up Jewish. Both my parents were Jewish, kept a kosher house, observed the high holidays, spoke Yiddish when I wasn't supposed to know what they were saying, and had some way of defining people who were not Jewish so that I learned that I was "us."

I didn't say prayers, in fact I thought that "they" said prayers, not "us." I didn't think that saying prayers was part of the Jewish tradition, and thinking about that now, I think it was that I was not told that I could pray for something material. The way I understood things, the prayers were given; he should live and be well, may he live 100 years, were the English versions, and then there were lots of things with the same inflection that were spoken in Yiddish, and I thought they were the same kind of prayers. They were the prayers of a group; it was an attitude that I was given because I was Jewish which didn't include asking God for things, and since most of the kids on my block were Catholic, and they went to church and were confirmed and communed, and prayed for things, I mistook that for Spirit. I thought they had it and I didn't.

Glenn was my guide to the door of the spirit. He told me that there was spirit, it existed, and it was obvious that he was telling the truth because he was happy. He enjoyed life. His programming job was mastered so he only had to give it 30 minutes a week. He used his available time to figure out how to build Isolation Tanks, and sculpt, and dance . . . and he told me that he wanted to introduce me to one of his most important guides, John Lilly.

We were in the dining room at Esalen Institute in Big Sur, California and Glenn began walking towards a man in a rumpled navy blue jumpsuit with the sleeves rolled up. He was smiling towards Glenn as if saying ,"Cmon over and say hello." I can still see him vividly at that moment. His blue eyes seemed piercing and purposeful, and he responded immediately to Glenn's introduction with, "this one has brains." Contact was made.

There were so many times that I didn't understand what he was talking about. He used an unknown to me vocabulary, and boy! did I feel dumb. But what I did understand gave me the frame to hang my Self on. It's a good thing that one of his strong lessons was in what he called, "Overvaluation Space." (Placing someone on a pedestal.)

He encouraged our work with the tank. His way of encouragment was to turn everything about the tank and its use out in the world over to us. He gave us the specifications for the tank, he referred requests for information about the tank to us, he said we should not program people before they used the tank (and admitted that was his program), he gave us the name "Samadhi," and he waved goodby with that odd smile of someone who has unloaded what seems like a desirable and attractive job on an eager and naive sucker.

Every time we were together he would tell us tank stories like the one about Richard Feynman at CalTech that is told in the first chapter, describe his wished for, ultimate tank experience as being outdoors in a round, see-through top tank, under a dark, starry sky. He said there should be tanks in hospital emergency rooms so that people who came in with a problem they couldn't exactly describe or define could go into the tank to find out exactly what was wrong. And he always asked us how things were going in "Samadhi," and teased us about whatever we answered.

In the group, we were the "Samadhi" people, the tank people. We took our place in that circle and what I think happened to me and everyone else in the circle was that being in the presence of John Lilly was the potent force that altered us more than anything else. He passed on to us an assignment to bring his invention, "The Isolation Tank," to the outside world. He said, "I was very lucky and privileged to be the first human to enter the tank domains. There was no literature to program my inperiences; no one more knowledgeable than myself to advise or teach me. I was really free!"

Glenn and I accepted the assignment and the cost has been to service the needs of all those who wanted and needed to work with the isolation tank.

We worked to provide freedom for all who came to the tank and that path provided us with never ending possibilities. We learned and leaped sometimes, but most of the time we did it the other way around. We introduced the isolation tank to tens of thousands of people, which required that we build an industry, which required us to take many risks, which led to many mistakes AND many successes. Get the picture?

AND THEN, we met John Lilly's friend, E.J. Gold.

John Lilly proclaimed to the universe in the forward to E.J.Gold's classic *The American Book of the Dead*, "Here in short form is the substance of basic human esoteric teachings given in modern language."

E.J. Gold's modern language in books and speech is brilliant, provocative, encyclopedic and hilarious, often all at the same time. We were servicing his tank and were given some audiotapes of a workshop he gave on tanks in 1976. Although I had been in the business for years and am a recognized source person about floatation tanks, these talks "got" me. I had forgotten that I might get out of the tank in a different universe than the one surrounding the tank I entered. The bottom of the next level appeared. Just as I wanted the floatation tank out there for everyone, I wanted these talks out there for everyone. I was given permission to edit them for release in this book. Twice I sat at a dinner table with John Lilly and E.J. Gold in a very alive dining room. This book formed in my imagination as another meeting of these two friends talking about my favorite subject.

Please consider what it says carefully.

Lee Perry
October, 1995

Thanks For the Hallucinations,

Dr. Lilly

The first time that I met Richard Feynman I had heard that he was giving some lectures at the Hughes Research Laboratory in Malibu through a friend of mine and they were going to be at 3:00 PM on a Wednesday afternoon. Approximately five of us went down there: myself, Toni, and several friends to attend these lectures on quantum mechanics. We arrived at the front desk at Hughes Research Laboratory, and there was a very nice receptionist who asked us what we wanted. We said we wanted to hear Professor Feynman's lectures. There was a character leaning over the counter on the right. He had been talking to the receptionist and he listened to me for a few minutes and then he said, I thought he was the janitor actually, "Well you know Professor Feynman has been lecturing for some weeks on this subject and you may not be able to understand what he is saying."

I said, "That doesn't bother me at all. I want to hear his lectures."

So then Toni who was there with me caught on to who this really was and looked up at him and said,"Are you Professor Feynman?"

He said,"Yes." So during the next fifteen minutes I proselytized him, and it only took fifteen minutes, I timed it. We got there at 20 minutes to three and his lecture was due at three, so I had fifteen minutes to convince him that he ought to go into the tank and much to my surprise he arranged to be at our house the next Wednesday at 9:30 AM. For twelve weeks he came faithfully every Wednesday morning, got in the tank for two hours, had lunch with whoever was there, and then we all went down to his lectures.

At his lectures he asked some of the girls who were with us how it happened that they came to these lectures. He thought they couldn't possibly be understanding what was going on, and these girls said that he didn't realize how entertaining he is when he is lecturing, and he is, as you all know.

During that twelve weeks, Dr. Feynman made progress. He sent me a copy of his book, *Feynman on Physics* after the twelve weeks and he said,"To John Lilly with thanks for the hallucinations, Dick Feynman." We had of course some rather powerful teachers there also, and Baba Ram Dass showed up one day for lunch and he and Richard Feynman had quite a conversation, as you can well imagine.

The science of inner research as opposed to the science of outer research is something that has bothered me ever since I was rather young. My first scientific paper was written when I was sixteen years old and was entitled *Reality*. I made the distinction between the inner and the outer realities and just arbitrarily divided them. Of course there are rather sloppy

ς/2·31·87

E.J.Gold, *Where Are The Mice?*,
Pen and Ink, Rives BFK, 1987.

boundaries as you all know between your insides and your outsides, and I started investigating this in depth in 1954, when we did the first set of tank experiments; 1954 to 1956 was the initial period. We had a rather complex method of doing it. We had a face mask that covered the head with no eye holes, so you couldn't see out of it and then a very efficient breathing system with very low dead space and a valve system that was automatically balanced to the pressure that you were at in the water.

I found many things there that I didn't dare write about at the time because I was in the National Institute of Mental Health as one of the researchers rather than as one of the patients. My neighbors were all psychiatrists and they were all ready to jump on you at the drop of a hat about psychosis and possibly lock you up if you got too far out. I had very disciplined surroundings with a particular cast to them and I found in the tank that they were wrong but I didn't dare say so until much later.

In 1956 I wrote the first paper on the subject and reviewed the history of solitary sailors, of people who have lived in the Polar night alone, including Richard Byrd, Christian Rutter, and various other people. Those accounts bore out practically everything that I had experienced in the tank. I was able to say in the paper that these experiences were very common among people in solitude and I owned up to one little hallucination, or as we now call it, visual display. It is a much less loaded term. Hallucinations have the connotation that you get caught in them, and that you begin to believe them, not as if real but as real. At no time have I ever made that mistake in the tank. I have made that mistake outside the tank but not inside.

Over the years, we have now been working 21 years

with tanks, everywhere I went I had to build another tank. I had one in the Virgin Islands, one in Miami, one in Baltimore and so on, one at Esalen. The one at Esalen was never finished. It was being built over a year but somehow the enthusiasm for building it disappeared at that time. Then when I went to Chile, I just had a black box that I could get into to escape the rest of the group.

I find it is absolutely essential every day to have some solitude, to have, if you can't make it in a tank, at least have solitude in a room and to meditate or do whatever it is one has to do to recharge the battery.

Now the tank got a reputation in the early years because the Director of the National Institutes of Mental Health needed to increase his budget and so he told the Senate that we were working on brain washing. For the reputation of the tank it turned out that this was very good because that meant that nobody wanted to be a subject in it and everybody got the horrors at the very thought of climbing into a box and going into the silence and darkness, so I was able to really be in solitude. They all stayed away from me. In the early years of research that sometimes is good. In this particular case it worked very well. When I gave my first paper to the psychiatrists, (it was in one of the psychiatric journals eventually) there was this big panel of discussants of my paper. Most imposing. They speculated about all these things and tried to weave them into the usual psychiatric theories about hallucination and regression and all of these other things. Luckily I had been through the mill in psychoanalysis, spent eight years on that one, both in training analysis and analyzing others, so I knew the jargon. I knew the theories they were working on and in the tank they didn't work at all. Phenomena began to appear which in psychoanalysis you can only explain by the

technical term, "Regression in the service of the ego." Now if
that isn't a cop out I don't know what is. In other words you
can go back into your own past history as it were, and identify
with it and regress. Well, that's a put down. Actually when
you get in the tank you find that the intact adult is always
there, that every bit of knowledge that you have stays with
you and nothing goes flying out the windows as if you are
psychotic.

　　Jay Shurley and I, he was my second subject, he set up
a tank in Oklahoma, but he escaped from my influence and I
noticed that he was calling me a symptom psychotic also
later. That's the trouble with psychiatrists, they revert to type
as soon as they get away from you.

　　He and I wrote a paper together which was published
in 1961, by Columbia University Press on the psychophysi-
ological aspects of space flight. It is rather amusing as to why
it was published there. That wasn't our first choice. Our first
choice was a symposium at Harvard which later became
known as the Sensory Deprivation Symposium.We apparently
were thorns at that meeting because every speaker that got up,
and there were about nine speakers who had done so, called,
"Sensory Deprivation Research," we asked them just two
questions:

　　Number one, did the investigators themselves go
through the procedure?

　　Number two, did any of the subjects ask for a second
run? These are the key questions. The answer to the first one
in all nine cases was no, none of the researchers had been
through it. Now others had. These were all psychiatrists. Then
the answer to the next question was also no.

　　Shurley and I both found that we got addicted to tank
work rather than being repelled by it. We got quite attached to

the tank and we thoroughly enjoyed the experience every time. So we were wondering where the hookers were in the other work and so we started looking at the other work more carefully. Jay and I both had decided that we were going to remove all noxious stimulation because when you are isolated, floating in the darkness and silence, the last remaining stimulus is the one that does the programming. If you have a low level pain due to back position or neck, or something of this sort, that colors your experience. It is as if these survival systems built into our brain having to do with pain have a subtle programmatic effect which you then tend to project onto the particular experiment, onto the experience.

In reviewing other people's work, we found that they were having people lie on a bed for example, or in a poliomyelitis respirator, or just sit in a chair in a black room for many hours. Or they were putting cuffs on the subjects' arms and a white mask over their face with a bright light shining on it and adding white noise to the room.

Well I don't blame these people for freaking out and not coming back. I had been through some of that work with Hebbs' group in Montreal where I went to visit after I had completed the first year or so of what we were doing and found that they were not correcting for the pain that ultimately leads to bedsores, for example. They were insisting that their subjects lie in a particular position for hours on end. Well this ultimately, as anybody who has been in a hospital knows, leads to problems and it colors the kinds of experience that the person has.

Jay and I made sure that any support was of surgical rubber and spread over a very large area of the body so as to cut down the stimulation. We had no problem with circulation of blood through the skin or any of these other things that other people had. So sensory deprivation got a bad name in general and I noticed in the latest issue of the *American Scientist* that one of the researchers has finally come out and said it doesn't necessarily have to be unpleasant. They are finally beginning to change in the field.

We knew from the beginning that solitude, isolation and confinement can be pleasureable, or you can make it into anything you wish. If you are upset you can calm yourself down there, or if you are one of the far out people that has a lot of talent, you can get out of your body or whatever else you are going to do there and know that the body is safe.

We now have modified the system so that it is incredibly safer than it was. I had been worried about the possibility of drowning. When we had the mask for example, one of the tubes leaked and I started to breathe water. One of the air tubes sprung a leak and I breathed water and before I knew what was happening I was standing outside, beside the tank with the mask off and I didn't know what happened in the transition. It all happened so fast that there was no recording of it, but I didn't worry too much from that point on about my automatic survival mechanisms. They would take over the whole show leaving me out of it, and if you have that kind of faith in your own ability to survive you can handle these situations much more easily. Because of that kind of experience and because a head mask had to be tailored to the particular person's features, we finally decided that this was too ponderous.

In St. Thomas I kept the mask for a while. I had an eight foot cube of sea water insulated, kept at 93 °F. I was suspended in the middle with a mask on, but I quickly found that sea water increased my buoyancy to a point where I didn't need the mask because I could float on my back at the surface and my legs went down and my arms went down, they were heavy. My head tended to fall back into the water, but if I put my hands at the back of my head and crossed my fingers in the back, I could stay there indefinitely and I spent several hundreds of hours during a two year period in 1964 to 1966 in the tank. When we set the tanks up at Malibu, I decided to try an idea that I had gotten onto and that was just keep adding salt to the water until we got a density high enough so that the whole body floated. We started out with sodium chloride and made the solution dense enough so that everyone floated. Now the trouble with sodium chloride is that if you have the slightest cut or any sort of lesion on your skin it's incredibly uncomfortable and stays that way. We had to coat ourselves with silicone and various other ointments that you can get at the drugstore that repel water. We decided to go back to sea salt so we bought bags of sea salt and tried that. Well this was still irritating. So then we began to think about it and we used an old remedy that people have known about for years and which is another component of the sea salt other than the sodium chloride and that's magnesium sulphate. You can purchase this but the trouble with it is that the formula is, $MgSO_4.7H_2O$, so you are buying a lot of water, which is a kind of waste, but if you try and buy the dry $MgSO_4$ without the water, the expense goes up astronomically.

Finally we arrived at the point where we put 500 pounds in a tank about seven feet long and four feet wide in which the water is ten inches deep. This solution then turned out to be non irritating. If you have a small cut, there is a stinging when you first get in the water, but pretty soon the magnesium ions apparently calm down the nerve fibers at the end the way calcium does, and you are no longer irritated at those locations and you can go on for hours without any skin

5. 12.88

E.J.Gold, *Queen of the Hall,*
Pen and Ink, Rives BFK, 1987.

irritation whatsoever. So we have a sort of anesthetic solution for local lesions and it is of high density. The density is high enough so that the skinniest person floats, the hands, feet, and head float.

The first tanks built here in Los Angeles by Glenn Perry, the Samadhi Tank Company, you had to climb over about a four foot wall to get into it. Well this stalled many subjects, especially those with short legs. Now we have the door opening just above the surface of the water and you can just step right in.

This modification was made after I had a bicycle accident and broke a lot of bones. I came back from the hospital and wanted to go into the tank to see what would happen. I found that all of the pain that I had holding the shoulder up under gravity disappeared as I was floating and for the first time I could move my arm comfortably to its limits. So the tank has several other uses than the ones we have been putting it to, but the main one that I want to emphasize is rest. You can float in the tank and rest faster than any other way that I have ever experienced. Now why is this?

When you are not working under gravity holding the body upright, all of the receptor organs and the central nervous system parts which are calculating constantly the direction of gravity have ceased their activity and can be used for other purposes. What most people find is when they get into the tank there are sensations of apparent movement, the overshoot from having been under gravity but the body isn't moving. It is as if the simulation of your body is moving so you can feel as if you are constantly going over a waterfall but you are not moving at all. If you sit down in the tank and then lie down fast and float you can get this sensation of continuing to go over and over, or you can get rotating on

E.J. Gold, *Somersault,*
Pen and Ink, Rives BFK, 1987.

some axis, either perpendicular to your body or along the length of your body, and this simulation of your body then rotates, but you know that the body itself is fixed. This kind of thing I have never experienced outside the tank. There are other things that happen.

Any one of the sense systems can begin to display activity to you, either visual or acoustic or skin sensations or deep inside sensations. This spontaneous sort of activity that starts can develop to extreme conditions in which you believe that you are going through an experience in which your body is not in a tank and you are somewhere else, but you are totally there.

Tank experiences have been compared to LSD, mescaline, peyote experiences, and so forth. All I can say is that it is a very, very different experience. I've done LSD back in 1964 when it was legal. I took LSD and went into the tank in St. Thomas, and I must say it is an entirely different kind of experience. It is as if the drug limited you, constricted you. Now it is true that you can move into places you are not allowed to go in, you did not allow yourself to go into before as it were, as if a small level of randomness in the neuronal events in your brain was added by the prescence of the drug. Actually you are constricted in the sense that you have added noise to the system in which you are the resident.

First I did ten years of tank work without acid even though there were a lot of pushers on the staff at NIMH (National Institutes of Mental Health) who wanted me to take it in the tank, and I refused because I didn't want to contaminate the experience by any such means. I stayed away from acid for ten years, and then in 1964 I had an opportunity to do it legally and did it and spent two years studying what happened.

In spite of Leary and many other people who have said

that LSD expands your consciousness, I don't think it does. I think what it does is to constrict consciousness and make it as it were into a searchlight beam in a certain set of directions so you can break through into spaces you couldn't break through before. If you can do the same thing without it, say by means of meditation or just plain tank work or just working on yourself, whatever it is that you have to do in order to change your state of being in this direction, then you can see the difference. Without the drug you have full peripheral vision as it were. You have full hearing and a full presence and you know everything that you know outside that situation, so it has the same advantages that meditation does. It gives you a very broad consciousness that is unimpaired   and unchanged in the sense of consciousness itself.

     Now these days, we hear a lot about altered states of consciousness. Well as far as I am concerned there are two mistakes in that. Number one, the word altered. My aunt had a cat that she had altered, so if you want to call these castrated states of consciousness, okay. But then the second error is, so far as I am concerned, there are only two states of consciousness— conscious and unconscious and that's it. Consciousness of itself is a very mobile, frisky sort of a creature and it does not acknowledge any changes in state other than being shut off. I would prefer the term state of being and not altered state of being, but just state of being and so I like to talk about states of being. States of consciousness you could symbolize by SOC and states of being by SOB — so it's easy to remember.

The Directions Are In The Glove Compartment

Who doesn't know what the isolation tank is?

It's a box of water that's 10 inches deep, so you can float. It's got an epsom salt solution with a density of 1.25, which means you have 800 pounds of epsom salts. You float in this, even your head floats. The head density is about 1.15, something like that in most people. But you have to remember that the center of buoyancy, and the center of gravity of the head are at about the same place, allowing you to tilt your head back comfortably without fear of sinking.

The temperature of the water is kept at $93.5\ ^0$ F, and the air above it is kept near saturation. A very small, quiet, air pump keeps fresh air moving through the tank.

Personally, I don't like the idea of anything moving while I am in the tank, I don't like any source of stimulation like that. The heat comes from a heater under the bottom of the vinyl liner, and there is a very accurate thermostat that holds the temperature to a tenth of a degree. A filter pump turned on after leaving the tank cleans the water between floats.

All right now, if you work in the tank, what you're doing is shutting down all the known senses, insofar as you can. You cut out all the light. If you're lucky and you have a remote location, the sound (except for very low frequency from airplanes) is imperceptible. Sound is the hardest thing to handle.

The temperature is more or less isothermal over the body's surface, and you find when you get out of the tank that one of the major sources of stimulation in humans is the temperature gradient changes on the body surface. This is an incredibly powerful thing, but you don't realize it until you've been exposed to an isothermal environment like this for several hours.

So by attenuating vision, hearing and the propriocep-tive sense, and floating at the surface so that the gravitational field is reduced to the minimum, you can relax every single muscle. Even your ear muscles, your neck muscles, your hands, your arms, your back, and so on. You can find the areas where you're holding needlessly, and you can let go. Once you do this, and go through all this, and get the inputs to the brain down to the minimum possible, you then suddenly realize that that is what has tied you to consensus reality, and now you're free to go.

I began the experiments with physical isolation when I was with NIMH, (National Institutes of Mental Health) in Washington. In neurophysiology there had long been a ques-tion of what keeps the brain going. Where are its energy sources? One obvious answer was that the energy sources are

E.J. Gold, *Dancing Cheek to Cheek*,
Pen and Ink, Rives BFK, 1987

strictly biological and internal and they do not depend on the outside environment. But some people were arguing that if you cut off all stimuli to the brain it would go to sleep. So we decided to test this hypothesis. This was easily done by creating an environment in a tank that would isolate a person from external stimuli. For a couple of years I periodically immersed myself in the tank and studied my states of consciousness. There you can forget your body and concentrate on the working of your mind.

The first thing you get is physiological rest. You're free of gravity; you don't have any more of those gravity computations that you do all day long. Finding where gravity is, and in what direction, and computing how you can move and not fall takes up about 90% of your neural activity. As soon as you start floating you're freed of all the gravity computations you've been doing all the time, so you find you have a vast piece of machinery that was being used for something else and you can now use it for your own purposes. For example, you can instantly feel that you are in a gravity-free field. It's as if you are somewhere between the moon and the earth, floating, and there's no pull on you. As soon as you move, of course, you know where you are, but if you don't move, your environment disappears and, in fact, your body can disappear. I credit my nine books to ideas generated in the tank. Since reality is a matter of local custom, the way I see it, whatever you believe to be true becomes true in the tank.

All the average person has to do is to get into the tank in the darkness and silence and float around until he realizes he is programming everything that is happening inside his head. You are free of the physical world at that point and anything can happen inside your head because everything is governed by the laws of thought rather than the laws of the

external world. So you can go to the limits of your concep-
tions. When you are floating in the tank you are certain of the
reality of what you are experiencing. I started off with the
notion that I was creating everything I experienced. But a lot
of things happened that made me ask some radical questions
about the nature of reality and different modes of perception.
I began then to see that interpreting all the novel experiences
in the tank as projections was an arrogant assumption. For
example: I went through an experience in which another
person I knew apparently joined me in the dark, silent environment of the tank. I could actually see, feel and hear her. At
other times I apparently tuned in on networks of communication from other civilizations in other galaxies. I experienced
parking my body and traveling to different places.

It was not psychosis I was exploring in the tank, but
belief structures. I was examining the way in which we program our beliefs and impose limits on what we may perceive
and experience by these beliefs. I wanted to know what
principles were governing the human mind. If we consider the
human mind as a kind of computer, I was looking for the
basic programs which were built into the computer and the
meta-programs which we impose upon the mind by conscious
choice or unconscious compulsion. I wanted to discover how
many of the meta-programs could be raised to the conscious
level and be changed, or reprogrammed. That became the
thesis of my most important book, *Programming and Meta-
Programming of The Human Bio-Computer.*

After 10 years in the tank I formulated a working rule:
Whatever one believes to be true either is true or becomes
true in one's own mind, within limits to be determined experi-
mentally and experientially. These limits themselves are, in
turn, beliefs to be transcended. The limits of one's beliefs set

the boundaries for possible experience. So every time you
reach a limiting belief it must be examined and gone beyond.
For the explorer there are no final true beliefs.

Compulsion is being trapped in a known psychic
reality, a dead-end space. Freedom is in the unknown. If you
believe there is an unknown everywhere in your own body, in
your relationships with other people, in political institutions,
in the universe, then you have maximum freedom. If you can
examine old beliefs and realize they are limits to be overcome
and can also realize you don't have to have a belief about
something you don't yet know anything about, you are free.
My book, *The Center of The Cyclone,* deals with the rules for
exploring the inner-outer spaces of consciousness. The basic
skill is one that has been known since ancient times. In yoga
and in Eastern thought it is the equivalent of establishing the
fair witness or the witnessing self. I think of it as one
becoming an observer and watching the operation of the
programs which are governing one's thinking and behavior:
to pull out of an experience, step back, and watch the
program.

Much of psychoanalysis involves gaining this skill of
seeing how you have gotten trapped in the past with some
program that solved a problem in childhood, but was over-
generalized and carried forward and has continued to operate
in inappropriate situations.

Tremendous energy is locked up in the old programs,
or what Jung called "autonomous complexes." One can release the energy with enough distance from the emotional
involvement in the programs. One must see them like an old
movie on T.V., or hear as a tape that you have heard a thousand times with the realization that you are not the programmer and you are not that which is programmed and you are

11-27-87

E.J.Gold, *Where's The Sofa?*,
Pen and Ink, Rives BFK, 1987.

not the program. Your identity becomes established as an independent agent. Once this ability to disidentify yourself from old programs, programming and from the programmer becomes generalized, you have the key to higher states of consciousness. By refusing to identify with the programs you transcend them and gain a measure of control. In this way you begin to exercise the meta-programming powers of the human bio-computer, the ability to create self-consciously the principles that govern thought and behavior.

We are approaching a marriage between the modern scientific point of view and the old esoteric and mystical knowledge. Now we are exploring new modes of access to states of consciousness which have been experienced for centuries. It is an empirical approach to those dimensions of consciousness that Eastern thinkers spoke of as levels of enlightenment or satori. I will elaborate a series of maps and some rules of the road.

The most helpful one for me was developed by Oscar Ichazo, the master who ran the school in Chile in which I spent eight months. He assigns numbers that relate to the length and frequency of sound waves to characterize the different levels of consciousness.

Level 48 is the rational, neutral state at which your mind is operating efficiently but without emotion.

Level 24. The experience of different types of Satori, or enlightenment, begin at level 24. Level 24 involves enjoyment in doing some activity that is done well and without conflict. This is the professional satori, the state of integrated work.

Level 12. As we move up in the scale to level 12 we reach a state of blissful awareness. At level 12 you can't function smoothly in the world because you are in bliss. You still are in your body but the usually inanimate reality around you seems alive and animated. At this level it is frequently difficult to speak. You accept the here and now. Sometimes this state can be reached in sexual intercourse. It is also the kind of enlightenment Zen speaks about.

Level 6. Moving up to level 6 you get out of your body for the first time. You become a point of consciousness, love, energy, warmth, cognition. This point is mobile. It can travel inside your body or into outer spaces. You still have your own "I," your center of consciousness, but your body is not experienced.

Level 3. The highest level of satori from which people return, the point of consciousness becomes a surface or a solid which extends throughout the whole known universe. This used to be called fusion with the Universal Mind or God. In more modern terms you have done a mathematical trans-formation in which your center of consciousness has ceased to be a traveling point and has become a surface or solid of consciousness. Here you lose the "I" almost completely, although some memory of this state is retained after reentry to consensus reality. It was in this state that I experienced "my-self" as melded and intertwined with hundreds of billions of other beings in a thin sheet of consciousness that was distrib-uted around the galaxy. A *membrain.*

You can program yourself to move into any space you know exists if you use discipline and concentration.

This is the most turned-on country the world has ever seen. The rest of the world is way behind. Our kids are turned on to levels of consciousness and possibilities of travel into mental and spiritual spaces in an unprecedented way. But the people I am most interested in are the successful heads of corporations and bureaucracies. Many of these people already

E.J.Gold, *Restful Peace,*
Pen and Ink, Rives BFK, 1987

operate at the level of satori 24. They are joyfully locked into their work. But they have never had maps which suggested to them the possibility of achieving more blissful levels of consciousness. What might happen if they could visualize the possibility of spending the weekend in satori 12, or even of achieving satori 3, in which they would realize that their essences are hooked to every other essence in the whole universe? It might turn out that exploring the far-out spaces of human consciousness is the fastest way to social transformation.

Now, if we assume, as I expressed in *The Scientist,* that somehow or another we, as a being, are not necessarily generated by the brain structure but that we came from somewhere else and take over a brain as it were, then we have the opportunity of leaving it, à la Robert Monroe's *Journeys Out of the Body* and various others who astral travel. Perhaps we are not necessarily fixed to the brain—and we can experience this in states of coma and states of anesthesia and states of insult to brain structure. In going back through some of the material about my own birth, I realized that I did get out and watch my mother struggling with producing the vehicle that I was going to inhabit. That's recounted in *The Scientist.* I got stuck in that stage of labor before the cervix opened, and there was a crushing purple-red force. The whole universe was collapsing on my being, and then, suddenly, I was released out of that. I never experienced the release point in my mature work. It was blocked. But while I was watching a movie of Russian waterbabies, I suddenly saw that birth is a joyful release from boredom. I remember now my own boredom before the stage of compression started. Somehow or other the richness increases suddenly after you're out. Birth is a relief from intrauterine boredom. So, as far as I'm concerned, the only mortal sin left is, "Thou shalt not bore God."

You can see alternate realities in the visual sphere. The big test that you can do with this is, if you have a very dim light in the tank, that you can open your eyes and see whatever it is in the tank, close your eyes and see the alternate reality, open your eyes and begin to see the alternate reality and the external consensus reality at the same time. I'd like to see some psychophysics done on this to find out how bright those alternate realities are compared to external visual stimulus. I think that can be done.

This makes me think that the leaky brain [see *The Deep Self* for this theory— Editor] has several unknown channels of information coming into it, whether it's a baby that's being gestated in the womb or whether it's an adult investigation in the tank, this is taking place in the lower levels of awareness and they are operating all the time.

Now, in the womb you have a situation like that of the tank, so, late in gestation, the baby may be seeing alternate realities, and this may be the memories that we have after we are born. It may also be some of the dream world that we can evoke later. I'm just throwing these things out as a possible theory.

There is the analog of end organs (structures forming the end of neural paths consisting of effectors or receptors with associated nerve terminations) within the brain which are sensitive to quantum mechanical radiations of various sorts that are present beyond our conscious instrumentation. The only instrument that can detect these subtleties is in the brain. If you go in the tank with that theory, you then have something which is extremely valuable, and that is the ability to program into alternate realities. You may be sucked into one that you didn't want to be in, and you may panic and get stuck there, and then you begin to think about it, relax and let go, and then a new one will come up like a new movie or a new experience.

At NIMH, I devised the isolation tank. I found the isolation tank was a hole in the universe; I gradually began to see through to another reality. It scared me. I didn't know about alternate realities at that time, but I was experiencing them right and left. You're safe in the tank because you're not walking around and falling down, or mutating your perception of external "reality."

The experience of higher states of consciousness, or alternate realities—is the only way to escape our brain's destructive programming, fed to us as children by a disgruntled karmic history. Newborns are connected to the divine; war is the result of our programmed disconnection from divine sources.

I am writing a book about alternate realities called *From Here To Alternity: A Manual on Ways of Amusing God.* I have experienced states in which I can contact the creators of the universe, as well as the local creative controllers — the Earth Coincidence Control Office, or ECCO.

They're the ones who run the earth and program us, though we are not aware of it. When I asked them, "What's your major program?" they answered, "To make you people evolve to the next levels, to teach you, to kick you in the pants when necessary."

Because our consensus reality programs us in certain destructive directions, we must experience other realities in order to know we have choices. That's what I call Alternity. I can open my eyes in this reality and dimly see the alternate reality, then close my eyes, and the alternate reality picks up. You can tune your internal eyes. They are not what is called

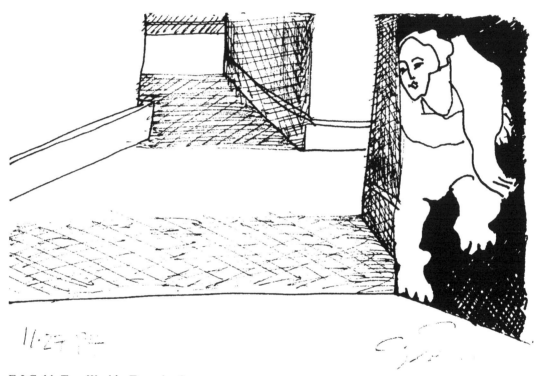

E.J.Gold, *Two Worlds, Turn the Corner,*
Pen and Ink, Rives BFK, 1987.

the "third eye," which is centrally located, but in stereo, like the merging of our two eyes' images. Perhaps someday, if we learn about the type of radiation coming through those eyes, we can simulate the experience with a hallucinatory movie camera—an alternate reality camera. Wheeler's hyperspace from within.

Wheeler's hyperspace also is known as a "nonlocal reality." Each of a pair of photons coming from an atom knows immediately what the other is doing, no matter how far away from each other they are. You can assume the existence of tachyons—faster-than-light-particles, carrying messages— but I prefer Bell's theorem solution to the Einstein-Podolski- Rosen experiment (which illustrated a seemingly impossible connectedness between particles in two different places). According to Bell's theorem, hyperspace would be a region of hidden variable in which all realities are represented at a single point and in which there is no need for messages to travel. The "hyperspace" with which I've been working is one in which I can jump from one universe to another—from this reality to an alternate reality—while maintaining human structure, size, concepts, and memories. My center of con- sciousness is here, and I can know immediately what's going on anywhere in the universe. It's a domain I now call Alternity, where all choices are possible.

My experiences have convinced me that Eastern yoga philosophy is right: that there is a *purusha* or *atman* (soul) for each person—one for the planet, one for the galaxy, and so on. As mathematician/philosopher Franklin Merrell-Wolff says in his book, *The Philosophy of Consciousness Without an Object,* consciousness was first—before the void even. When consciousness got bored and turned in upon itself, becoming conscious of itself, creation began. He/ she/ it created time, space, energy, matter, male, female—the whole tableau. It all got so complicated that sneaky things may go on beyond its ken.

If you get into these spaces at all, you must forget about them when you come back. You must forget you're omnipotent and omniscient and take the game seriously so you'll engage in sex, have children, and participate in the whole human scenario. When you come back from a deep tank session—or coma or psychosis—there's always this extraterrestrial feeling. You have to read the directions in the glove compartment so you can run the human vehicle once more.

From Physics To Eastern Philosophy

You need a cerebral cortex of a critical size, with fine fiber connections running in both directions to lower systems. That's where the middle self ("I-me") lives, up in that cortex—not in the lower centers. The lower centers (our lower self) prod us from below, as it were, with love or hate or fear. I think that the superself controls from somewhere "above the brain," perhaps overview, perhaps Jane Roberts' oversoul, in the spiritual domains.

The preoptic nucleus in the anterior hypothalamus, at the base of the brain, is very negative. It's our main survival nucleus: If the temperature is too hot or too cold, this nucleus freaks out the rest of the brain. If there's too much sodium in the blood, it freaks out the brain. It's an area for total fear. Then, moving downward toward the spinal cord, you hit a part of the hypothalamus that stimulates extreme pain all over the body. If you move sideways in either direction in that area of the brain, however, stimulation becomes incredibly positive. Around the preoptic nucleus, you run into the sexual system which, in males, controls erection, orgasm, and ejaculation—each in a separate place— while farther back, in the mesencephalon, the three are integrated and fired off in sequence.

The brain has other pleasure systems, too—systems that stimulate nonsexual pleasure all over the body and systems that set off emotional pleasure. That is a kind of continuous pleasure that doesn't peak—a satori of mind. Satori and samadhi (terms for enlightened-bliss states in Zen Buddhism and Hinduism, respectively) and the Christian "states of grace" seem to involve a constant influx of pleasure and no orgasmic climax—like tantric sex. Spiritual states use these brain systems in their service. Many philosophers, including Patanjali, the second-century B.C. author of the Yoga Sutras, have said that jnana yoga—the yoga of the mind—is the highest form of yoga. In this self-transcendence one can experience bliss while performing God's work; only recently have I achieved this for days at a time.

Space and time as we know it are a function of matter and energy density. When the universe collapses, space, time and topology as we know it disappear. So a new topology, a new space, a new matter and a new energy all appear later. We happen to have gotten stuck in a narrow channel for now, but we don't have to be.

Where do we exist? If you follow Franklin Merrell-Wolff's *Philosophy of Consciousness Without an Object,* we only exist in superspace. Even so, you must realize that something of you is a connection with something of everything else in a super space or a hyper space which does not neces-

G/2·31·87

E.J. Gold, *Sunday Driver,*
Pen and Ink, Rives BFK, 1987

sarily need matter for its particular expression. These so-called higher states of consciousness are merely investigations of that ultimate non-material state.

Now if you've read *Center of the Cyclone,* I describe an experience in which I follow three cycles of the universe collapsing and re-expanding. There is an entity showing it to me. Man appears here, disappears there: the entity displays the whole cycle. Appears here and disappears there, appears here and disappears there, and so on through the three cycles. And I said "Where does Man go in the meantime?" And he said, "That's it." And I went into depression. I stayed in depression for six weeks, saying, "Is that all there is?" and then suddenly the realization came to me "I was out there with them. I'm one of us." And I went on a high, and I've been on it ever since.

I like Merrell-Wolff's statement that substantiality is inversely proportional to ponderability and refers to a being in "48 "(Ichazo's levels of consciousness system), looking at matter from the standpoint of the Planck length (6.624×10^{-27}) In other words the quantum observer, reduced to ten to the minus twenty seventh. There is no specification of present condition at that level. There is only the expression of potentiality in the future, and that potentiality is wide open. So that if a star collapses into a point, such as it does in a black hole, that whole star has gone. The matter of it has gone down to a size less than ten to the minus twenty-seventh centimeter. Now it's become indeterminate. Totally. It's not big enough to be determined, if you wish. So it can re-arise from that point in any form such as a universe like ours that lasts say twenty-five billion years, or a universe that lasts a millisecond, or a universe that lasts twenty five thousand years or twenty five million.

So the ultimate reduction that Wheeler has done, is that consciousness without an object is a total pool or reservoir for all possible universes. See now we're getting a much closer specification for the region of high density, which is everywhere. In you it's right in the middle of your head. It's in the presence of matter and the absence of matter. Matter as Wheeler says is like a cloud in the sky in relation to the earth or a cloud in the sky to the atmosphere. It makes very little difference.

And if you can reduce down to that pure self, there's an incredible space, or set of spaces, which I don't even want to begin to mention to you because I don't want to spoil your own adventure. All right. So if you look carefully at the way the brain's constructed, there is a fine fiber system that comes down to these critical nuclei and goes back to the cortex, and the fine fiber systems can modulate from down there, up here or from up here, down there.

So within yourself you do have at least the circuitry to exert control over these systems. You can create a sense of well-being, or you can create a sense of fear out of the operation of your own bio-computer. That's the most important message we have in regard to self meta-programming. I saw that in the tank.

I had done work with animals using electrodes, both dolphins and monkeys. I made a model of my own nervous system using that concept. I completed all those experiments on other animals and began to use the model on myself, and I suddenly realized that there are many controls filling the brain that won't allow you to push it beyond its circuit ceiling.

So fear and pain all have a ceiling and that is the big lesson in the tank as far as I am concerned. There is a ceiling to terror, and I can survive it in spite of a previous belief

E.J. Gold, *"C"*,
Pen and Ink, Rives BFK, 1987

system that I couldn't; I'm still here. I also found that pleasure could be created. At one point I went in the tank and said, "What's the maximum pleasure you can experience?"

Well, that period just before you blast in an orgasm. Not the orgasm itself, but just before that. So I worked on this, wrote down what I wanted to do, went in the tank, got up to just before orgasm, and when I got out of the tank I realized I had remained in that state for six hours. And I came back and I wrote in my notes, "So what?"

I mean you know, here is a demonstration of self metaprogramming in isolation, showing you that something or other in here was in control therefore could be in control.What is required is that something or other concentrate on being in control, that's what I learned. I also learned that if that something or other gave up control there could also be other states of consciousness in which control was an academic question.

Let's look at the connection with a space versus identification with a space. Ramana Maharshi long ago worked out an exercise. Sit quietly in solitude, or, with somebody who is compatible with what you're doing and ask, Who am I? Don't ask it in the verbal stream, as if out there. Ask it internally. Do not put it on a neon sign saying Who am I, question mark as if out there. It's inside. Who am I really? What is my true self? And then as an answer comes up spontaneously out of your unconscious, out of your pre-conscious, whatever, wherever it comes from, just throw it away. You say, I am not that. Here is an example. Who am I? John Lilly. Uh-uh. Because there are times when that body's non-existent. But I'm still existing. And so on.

You go right on through this, until finally you can see as you work on your onion, and peel layer after layer of identification off, you'll finally get down to a core, of who you really are, quote, for you. And you'll stop identifying with negative programs, you'll stop identifying with any programs, any meta-programs, and you'll realize that there is a pure self that doesn't have anything to do with the body , with the programming, the external reality, with anybody else, and so on.

This brings to mind a meta-program to work on that might allow you to experience a much wider range of consciousness than you are ordinarily willing to permit yourself. Find your particular doorway into the state. You have automatic programs which key in and say no, don't go into that state, as you start to enter it. I am pretty sure that each one of you has a few seconds of entry that occur, especially as you're falling asleep, or when you are drunk, or when you are totally fatigued and you must do something, or when you're making love, and so on. The important thing is to enlarge those few seconds into minutes and into hours, and to get the control. To take the narrow slot that you now have and widen it in time. Well, to view the material cybernetically, as soon as you construct something out of primordial parts which become interconnected, the new entity that is represented by that group of subentities, is something entirely new and different. Every neuron is hooked to at least five others. This interconnectivity in our cerebral cortex causes a whole new type of organization to occur that an ameoba does not have, and that an ant does not have because it doesn't have the interconnectedness over a sufficiently large population. So each level or number of interrelated, interlocked units, is different than all the previous smaller levels from which it evolved.

There are organisms on the planet that have brains

E.J.Gold, *Who's Calling?*
Pen and Ink, Rives BFK, 1987.

twice the size of ours. I have come up against Orca, that had a brain size three to four times the size of mine. Six thousand grams. If we are going to attempt to speed up evolution by playing around with brain size, maybe we better communicate with those who already have the large brains and find out what kind of programming we will have to put into our youngsters. Perhaps we could program computers to interconnect the number of humans necessary to link enough neurons to approximate the brain size of one Orca and establish a human committee to communicate with an Orca.

Well, let's talk about the simulation capacity of the computer. The size of the simulations, the number of them that can be held simultaneously is a function of the size of the total available number of units, whether neurons or micro-circuits, that are present with a sufficient inter-connectedness at a sufficient speed so that with our time frame, we can see it happening. Of course, we want to see something happening in our time frame. If we want to stretch to much longer time frames for a thinking process, conceive of our present simulation of the galaxy as an organism. Enlarge the brain structure to the size of the galaxy with comparable numbers of stars to neurons involved, with the proper radiation patterns, electromagnetic fields and so on. Now, imagine the time for the transmission of the signals for thinking to proceed, limited by the velocity of light. And now think, what is the thinking process of this huge organism with a life span of 20 billion years? Well, we've described that as evolution and that is incredibly slow to us. To it, we are incredibly fast. And we just come and go like that, and various other organisms like us come and go.

To approach another psychological oscillator we will talk about the theory of self-reference. There hasn't been a good theory of self-reference, in spite of the fact that psychology and various other disciplines keep talking about it. It took mathematicians an awfully long time to discover self reference and I think that it was due to the throttling influence of Aristotle.

Aristotle devised a logic which was non self-referential and did not contain time. So classical logic says, "This is true, that is false," but it does not say that "First this is true, then it is false, and then it is true." In other words then, there are no sequential states in classical logic. It's all absolutist. Absolutely true, or absolutely false and nothing in between.

Now this is convenient as the basis for the binary counting system used in computers, but once you construct a computer using this system, you suddenly run into self—referential circuits. And what do they do? They do all sorts of things. They can count, they can be used for time measurements, they can be used for logic, they can be used for oscillators.

Now let me give you an example of the kind of thing that classical logic cannot handle, in fact Whitehead and Russell said "no such sentences are to be allowed." The first one is very simple. Notice what this does to your state of mind. This sentence is false. Now, if the sentence is false, then what it says is true. But if what it says is true, then the sentence is false. So what the sentence does mentally, is set up an oscillation. True false, true false, true false. Whitehead and Russell called this the "Theory of Types" and threw such sentences out.

Now, what is the property of that sentence that allows it to be a psychological oscillator? It's self-referential. This sentence, referring to itself, is false. So that sort of thing could not be handled in those mathematics based upon classical logic.

Oxford mathematician G. Spencer Brown came along with *Laws of Form*, the first self-referential logic. By introducing a new set of concepts, all of which were so basic and so simple that most mathematicians couldn't understand what he was doing, he addressed this problem. Francisco Varella studied *Laws of Form* and said okay, we have a two valued system of logic here, let's make it three valued and put in special operators called self-referential operators. He came out with a new logic, which ostensibly and out front recognized self-reference. And the Varella operator solved the theoretical side of self-reference. However it didn't allow you to be quantitative yet. So Heinz Von Forrester appeared and took the Varella logic, and added to it, eigenfunction. *Eigen* translated from the German means self. Eigenfunctions are self-referential mathematical functions which tend toward stable points, stable values, called eigenvalues.

The eigenfunctions are very peculiar mathematical functions, in that they are dynamic. Let's start with a very simple one. Cosine $X = Y$; if you take any value of X and put it in that equation, calculate Y and then take the cosine of that Y, and calculate a new value for Y, and keep doing this, your cosine will always end up at a stable number, the eigenvalue, and in that case it's something like 43.7° (but you better do your calculations in radians rather than degrees; most calculators have to use the radians). If you take an additional cosine $X + X = Y$, this has multiple stable values.

And I worked on this in turn and used it in perception. Your eyes tend to operate by cosine $X + X = Y$. Let me illustrate. If you plug the value for 90° into that equation, the answer comes out $Y = 90°$. In other words it's an identity, a self-referential identity. But if you plug in 89°, the next value coming up will tend toward 90°. If you plug in 91°, it'll go back toward 90°, so there's a stable point towards which it tends to go. Now take 270° and plug it in. You plug in 270° and you get 270° out. But if you plug in 271° it'll go all the way back around to 90°.

So you can say that your nervous system, your eyes and head movements, tend towards the stable eigenvalue. If there's a noise over here, a click, and I turn towards it, my eigenfunction has moved the stable value towards what has disturbed me. So the self-referential system has operated in such a way as to respond to an outside, external reality stimulus, so that I can turn those organs for maximum recognition, maximum discrimination, towards the source of the disturbance. If there's a movement in my periphery I can turn and look and recognize what it is, even though in my periphery I can't recognize what that thing is. It could be a bug or a snake or a person. You can't recognize it. As soon as you turn you can see that it wasn't a snake, it was a person waving her arm. Any self-referential system alone, say you in the tank, is a closed system. Well, let us say that there's one theory that it's a closed system, and there's another theory that it's an open system. Let's take a look at the closed system theory first.

See how my beliefs are incredible. I refuse to get stuck with any one of them. There's always an alternate belief. That's an important belief to have. And what's the alternative to that? There's only one belief — to doubt many beliefs. There's only one truth. Everything I say is false. You see what the self-referential theory has done to me?

Say that you're in the tank, and assume you're a closed system. That can be pretty dull, because then you get involved in that mystery known as memory. And when you don't think of memory as being mysterious, but as just being a repetitious phenomenon that you'd like to get rid of — and you may be right, you should get rid of it — you've gotten caught in a self-referential loop which is acting as if it's stable, and hence, in my opinion, boring. We can look at this as a circle, and the two open ends of the circle where you make a cut are facing each other and there's stuff going right around that circle and that's your iterative process inside your own head. It's a hell of a state to be in in the tank, unless you enjoy that sort of thing.

All right. Now let's say that you're in a dyadic situation. And now try to represent the eigenfunction. Instead of these two ends being like this, you've opened it up, and this end goes around her circle or his circle and comes back in here, so now you've got a bigger circle — a dyadic one.

When you do that, that first circle we were talking about is cosine $X + X$; when you make two different eigenfunctions, and you combine them, you are adding them or multiplying them or doing anything else which combines them in some equation. It turns out that you have a whole new set of eigenvalues, of stable values. The solitudinous self-referential system, is a very different creature than the dyadic combination of that system with another one. Your mathematics now moves, to expand into a dyadic eigen-function and hence dyadic stable value. The stable values for you alone in solitude — and this is well known in the literature of solitude — change. The longer you are alone, in the wilds or in the mountains, the more your eigenvalues change. The more you are with one other person, there is a tendency at the beginning of the relationship for each to grasp the stable eigenvalues as quickly as possible and see if they apply in the dyadic situation. Battles over the stability equations aften occur in dyads because you can't do in a dyad what you can do in solitide.

G/2.31.87

E.J.Gold, *Wall Shy,*
Pen and Ink, Rive's BFK, 1987.

You can't do in solitude what you can do in a dyad.

Life is pretty dull if we have no surprises. We have surprises inside as well as outside. We try to teach people certain fundamentals about their own physiology and biology which are necessary for living on this planet. We call this the Planetside Trip, and then we show how one's ideas about external reality are carried over inappropriately into the internal reality of one's own mind.

We find that men who are active in the world tend to take the ideas they have derived from contacting other people in the external reality in general, and carry them in as rigorous programs inside their own heads. A certain amount of that is necessary for operating, but it isn't absolutely essential to do this all the time. So, when you get free within your own head, literally what you believe to be true is true, so long as there is no reference to the outside world, as long as you are immersed in your own cognitive reality.

Women are just the opposite. They tend to live inside, and they're quite content with their internal reality because they have worked it out more clearly than men in general. They go much more with their feelings and their states of being, and so they sometimes tend inappropriately to project the laws of the inner reality onto the external reality.

This is where we have so much abiding conflict between men and women, and each side thinks they know the truth. Well, each of them is only half there. And once they both discover that each of these regions is just as rewarding when you are free to move in them, the conflict ceases.

We have been answering the question of what happens to a brain and its contained mind in the relative absence of physical stimulation. In neurophysiology, this is one form of the question: freed of normal efferent and afferent activities does the activity of the brain soon become that of coma or sleep, or is there some inherent mechanism which keeps it going, a pacemaker of the "awake" type of activity?

Our minds are huge icebergs only 10% conscious, and the unconscious portion is beyond our immediate perception processes.

Once we learn to move inside, external senses and their representatives are a distraction. Get rid of the distractions as quickly as you can and go on with the interesting stuff. The interesting stuff is your states of being, and you can go through various kinds of transformation to your total state of being. As long as you don't hang onto blackness, or hang onto the silence, or hang onto the light, or hang onto any of these things, you ought to be able to look through all these phenomena.

My present use and experience of the tank is quite undramatic, restful, and restorative. As the second title of the book implies (*The Deep Self: Profound Relaxation and the Tank Isolation Technique*) my current goal and use is for the profound relaxation which I find very easy to allow in our tank.

Personally, I am no longer what I was when I was 21. My program now is that I'm an independent agent within this particular sphere, and I'm not necessarily tied to a particular brain, though every so often I take on that belief system if I'm talking to somebody. I try to get them to see alternatives to that belief system, and not necessarily just the Far Eastern one. There are science fiction ones. The point is to get the imagination free so that one can live out various scenarios and test out various ideas. That's the way I use the tank. The setting up of temporary scenarios — a temporary belief system — and then go with it without prediction.

5.1.2.88

E.J. Gold, *Care to Join Me?*,
Pen and Ink, Rives BFK, 1987.

Sanity Clause

There should be a sanity clause in the basic agreement when you enter the universe. You walk up to the desk:

You want to enter the universe?

Yes.

Okay, what's your purpose for being in the universe?

Oh, I just thought I'd hang out there for a while.

No, sorry, you've got to have a purpose.

Allright, let me see now, gosh I don't really have any purposes.

Oh well, fine, we'll just assign one to you.

Oh great, I'd appreciate that. I don't have anything to do for the next several trillion years.

Well, fine, sign right here and by the way there is a sanity clause in this.

A sanity clause, you mean if I fail to maintain my

sanity I have to leave the universe?

No, no, no, if for some reason you stumble upon and accidentally regain your sanity, you have to leave the universe.

Oh, well, is there anything to prevent me from accidentally doing that?

Oh, gosh, yes, a myriad of wonderful techniques are employed.

There's another case where someone's come out of the tank only a few feet and come as high as the God World, staggered out, looked at me and said,

What's going on? My God I got to get out of here. How will I ever get down from this? Oh, my God, where is everybody? I'm out of breath, I'm ready to pass out, look I'll see you around, okay? You know, I looked down and there's all these stars inside, how come the stars pass right through my body? Oh, my God, I got to get out of here .

In a couple of cases I say, You probably think this is all a dream, what's going on now. You probably think that you're dreaming about this stuff. But I want to remind you that you haven't been dreaming, and to prove it, I'll give you a sentence and the sentence is . . . (I don't want to tell you what the sentence is, because if I tell you what the sentence is I can't use it with you), and that will prove it. I'll tell   you about it if you come back out of this thing, and you think that this was a dream, and we talk about this later on at some point, perhaps in the Human World or wherever you happen to reconstitute, and then I'll give you the sentence and you'll know that it wasn't a dream after all.

In one incident I'm thinking about particularly, a woman went back, backed off from that and went into the Human World. About a year later I said, Well, was it a dream

S'/2.31.87

E.J.Gold, *Diving In,*
Pen and Ink, Rives BFK 1987

or wasn't it?

I remember that conversation where you said it wasn't going to be a dream. Didn't you say that there was a sentence that I could remember?

Yes, here's the sentence, and I told her the sentence.

Oh my goodness, it happened!

The thing about the human consciousness is that that's surprising.

Perhaps, if you were in the Jealous God world and you had the angelic or angel-demon view, if you wish to call it that, there isn't any word for it, particularly in the human language, devil is the closest word for that.

Djinn?

Djinn, that's a good one, the Djinn World is excellent. Why don't we call it the Djinn World? It would be so much better than calling it the Jealous God World, because Jealous God is not really true. It's not really a good name for it. The Djinn World is much better, thank you. Anyway, in the Djinn consciousness, you'd be damned surprised if it didn't happen, just the opposite to human consciousness in many ways. Human consciousness is very surprised if anything happens of a real nature. It's all supposed to be fake anyway. The closest thing to reality that humans experience is a movie. That's the most real thing that a human could do is watch a movie. I mean that's the closest to what it really is, so, humans haven't got a whole lot of reality going for them and neither do Djinn, necessarily. That wraps it up in terms of the Brute World on five dollars a day.

We haven't got time in a weekend seminar to deal with your habits and how they relate to what you are and what you do and why you do what you do and so on. You don't overcome habits. I just want to briefly sketch a few very basic things. I already mentioned that you are your habits, but I also want to point out to you that the habits which have been accumulated, more or less accidentally over a period of many billions and billions of years, and which have now created your Being, they can't be eliminated, but habits can be substituted for them which create in you conscious Beingness.

In other words, they create for you conscious life. However, you must realize if you undertake something like that, it's a matter of at least a twenty-year job because a habit isn't something you just do once. Many people think that they can create conscious habits in themselves by doing them for a few months or a few weeks, or even by doing them one time. Even a few years isn't enough to create a conscious habit, and habit doesn't necessarily mean a negative thing.

Don't think of a habit as something negative. A habit is just something that you have the tendency to do, and if you have a tendency to be unconscious, afraid, aggressive, attached to things in the world, envious, jealous, angry, frustrated, impatient, and unaware of your surroundings, of yourself, you have the habit to be an unconscious mechanical being. Those are habits which just accumulated through random action. You've collected those more or less the way a pack rat collects things. You collected them, not at all deliberately. As a result of that you see what you get. If you look at yourself right now, you're a result of arbitrary and random accumulation of habit. On the other hand, you can also have the habit to be a conscious Being, to live a conscious life, always and in everything, to live consciously no matter where you are, who you are and what you are. So, this is really a prime element that we're talking about. It's too bad that we can't really deliver that in a weekend. In other words, I would prefer to deliver that rather than a travel bureau. On the other hand, the travel bureau is more or less an indication of what's happening, it's more or less of an introduction to it, and it (maybe) puts you in the mood to get out of your habitual tendency to be a human — maybe even your habitual tendency to exist.

You know immortality is a lot in habit. It's a congenital habit of human beings to be immortal, and it's an unfortunate habit in the sense that it gets in your way, in terms of doing a lot of the things that really are enjoyable. If you knew what else was available to you, you wouldn't think human existence is that enjoyable or gratifying. Yes, gratification is the name of the game in the Human World. But why do you keep coming back? When you get to the gateway tank, you lie down and go into a separative state, into a second stage condition, then you come back into a first stage condition. You may have even gone to a fourth stage, then you come back to a third stage condition, and you reassemble the world and you wonder why. You walk out and see the sign that says, "Welcome to the Human World."

The reason for that is you have a habit of being human. That can't be solved in just one day. Understand that even if you make transference through the tank, your next rebirth will again be in the Human World, simply because you haven't conquered those habits which create in you the tendency to be a human.

There are 18 major habits that are called primary habits. These primary habits create unconsciousness and they create in you the tendency to be human. It's just a matter not of overcoming, because you can't eliminate, but of substituting for those 18 unconscious habits, 18 conscious habits.

You know for sure that your next rebirth will be human, so don't worry about it and you'll get back here even

E.J.Gold, *Am I Dreaming?*,
Pen and Ink, Rives BFK, 1987.

if you don't get back through the gateway. I mean, you'll get back through the gateway, but you may not know it.

Of course, you're explaining this by saying, I've come up to this mountain retreat and I've come up here for just a weekend and really, I've got to get back to work on Monday morning, I've got a terribly busy schedule ahead of me and so on, and explain it all that way. That is the Human World, that's what creates the Human World, why you think you're here and where you think you are. If you knew where you were right now, you probably wouldn't be so calm about it. It seems okay doesn't it? As long as it seems okay, it should be okay. Now, as I said, we can't deal with the major thing, that is overcoming all these habits that create in you the suffering, miserable, human creature, but we can overcome it to the degree that at least you can make a transference from one world to another through the gateways and do it more or less on an aware level. The way you do that is through the technique of categories.

I'll give you an example of categories: when you come into the Human World, the third stage, you sit there or stand there, however you do it, pace back and forth, fly, flip, float, maybe scrounge. I don't know what you do in there, what you think you do in there, but on your way back to the Human World you think,

Now, how can I come down off of this one? I'm as high as a dead goat. I've got to get down off this thing.

For one thing the cycles are too fast, they happen too often, and you can't think because you can't construct anything between cycles, you can't go across the cycles, everything intrinsically happens in one cycle. The kind of thinking that takes place isn't really thinking; it's perceiving the action of that cycle. To give you an example, in the beginning of the

second stage, first part of the second stage, you'd come out
with something like,

That light has got a. . ., and then the masks over there,
you know that mask over there is red, and the screen over
there is square, so anyway, as I was saying to so and so in the
chair. . . .

There's no connection. You don't remember having
seen the masks, you don't remember having talked about the
lights, you don't remember the screen, you don't remember
the chair, all you remember is the last thing, the thing you're
actually into at that point. So you can't think; because you
can't think you probably don't like it, and if you don't like it
you don't want to stay there, and if you don't want to stay
there you're going to start thinking of ways to get out.

If you have the habit to be human, the way you'll think
of this, you'll think you're so original, you'll say to yourself,
half-jokingly, for reasons known only to yourself,

I've got an idea.

Find a psychological and a physical explanation for
everything that's happening, and you will, and because you
do, you'll re-enter the Human World because you're thinking
in human categories. So you think in psychological and
physical terms. There has to be a psychological and a physical
explanation for everything. There's got to be a human explanation; the human thinks there's an explanation for everything.

A God doesn't need an explanation for anything.
Everything is self-explanatory, it is what it is because it is
what it is. It's raining because it's raining, not because there's
clouds in the sky or precipitation or because there's dust
motes and the water molecules gather around the dust motes
and fall. That's a Human World when that happens.

In the God World, if it rains, it rains because it rains. Now, in the Brute World, it rains because they're making it rain. You can get some idea of what's happening with that. In the Ghost World, it never rains; it never rains enough and if it does rain enough, it rains too much. In fact the Ghost World only has two sizes: too much and not enough. Now, in the Hell World occasionally it rains, but it rains because the soot carries the water down. If you've been to New York you have a reasonably pleasant view of what it is to be in the Hell World. Soot is everywhere. There's just ashes and soot falling from the sky all the time, and occasionally they happen to get clumps of water, and it's probably the purest water you'll drink there.

Anyway, in order to make the transference, you need to think in other categories and you'll have a categories session sometime. You're going to have a tank session and then you'll have a category session, or the reverse, and then you'll have another attempt at the gateway.

I'll give you a really fast example of the thing, I'll show you something. Now, that thing over there, what is it?

To a human what is this?

A microphone.

Okay, what else is it?

A club.

A club— there you go to the Brute World.

What is it to you?

A phallus.

Of course it is. What does it do? What is its use?

To procreate.

Of course, Brute World for you.

How about you? What is this?

It's a metal ice cream cone.

Of course it is. Djinn World.

If it's totally inedible, and you want an ice cream cone, then you've got the Hungry Ghosts.

How about you, what is this?

A microphone.

A microphone, welcome to the Human World.

What else is it besides a microphone? Invent another one.

It's a pressure system that only breathes in all the time.

That's right, of course it is, you're headed for the funny farm.

Certainly, it's obvious it's an interpersonal transmogrifier, you know what transmogrification is? It means to alter in a grotesque way, interpersonally transmogrify.

How about a wand or a sceptre?

Brute World for you.

Looks like some kind of spear.

No, but what is it, not what it looks like, what is it?

I don't know what it is.

Of course, you don't know what it is. Where are you going? If you don't know what it is, where are you going? You just don't know what it is!

Hell World?

Not necessarily, probably the Human World because the Human World is the world of exploration, wonder.

What is this?

It's a jewel.

Of course it's a jewel, anybody can see that, what kind of jewel?

Well, I saw it as a jewel made out of light, a crystal— like glass.

Wonderful, where's he going?

God World?

Sure, but you can't just have it here, you have to really know that this definitely is a jewel. It can't be a jewel and a microphone, it has to only be a jewel in order to go there.

It's a pocket traveller, it's a compact rocket and you hold onto one end and go.

Star Wars for you. I know what you are, I know exactly the civilization you're looking for. Unfortunately it's three hundred trillion years back. You can see it on *Star Trek.*

At any rate that's how you go about it, and I'd like you to have a short category session where you do that with some-one and Amaldo will do that with you. Are there any questions about what we've talked about? Briefly, because we have to end this talk pretty soon.

I'm going to point out something to you, now that we used the microphone. Lie down in the tank, and what are some of the things that occur? There are some very definite manifestations that occur. Think of those in utterly new cat-egories. Is water dropping from the ceiling, from the top, does it do that? Not so much anymore, does it? It doesn't do it nearly as much as it used to and the tanks all do that. There is a solution to that but it's not an excellent one, it's a partial solution, it works a little bit, and we're eventually going to work on getting a really good solution to that problem. How-ever, it shouldn't be a problem, a drop of something strikes you, but that's not a drop of anything, what is that really? Well, having read *The American Book of the Dead,* you obviously know what to do with that one, particularly if you can position your chest just under the drip, but of course it isn't a chest, is it? Then you have sensations, bodily sensa-tions, right? Think of those, not as bodily sensations, but think of them in an entirely new way.

So, let's say you have the experience of the water dropping on your chest, and you say no, that's not water dropping on the chest it's something else; I can't conceive of anything, so that determines the world that you want to go to. You could program that out to the world you want to go to, you could deliberately program the way that some do by taking this as a jewel and that as a cloud and this as . . ., or you could just come up with whatever you come up with.

Sometimes voyagers have tremendous trouble coming up with any explanation other than a human one. If you can't come up with another, invent a totally different thing. I definitely think you could work on that, you should work on that, and there are definite ways to work on it. It's offered, it's available.

At any rate, a lot of people get into the tank, lie down and try to overcome the sensations. They get stuck in the tank space and thinking about it. Wow, I'm moving around in this solution, I'm floating here in this tank and there's this vinyl wall over here, I just touched it. Now, I'm going to float over to the other one and touch the other vinyl wall. Well now, there's a drip coming down and I've got a crimp in my foot, my leg, my hand. I'm not breathing right. All of these come up. You think, if only I didn't have all these sensations, if I didn't have all of these perceptions and if I didn't feel all of this stuff going on, I'd be able to get out of here. Well, obviously you don't want to get out of there, you want to use everything proceeding in an entirely new way. By doing that you change yourself to some degree. You change what you are by what you believe. It not only becomes mentally true, it becomes physically true. I want you to understand that.

Talking about this, John has a saying, in the province

E.J. Gold, *One Step at a Time*,
Pen and Ink, Rives BFK, 1987.

of the mind, remember that thing? What you believe to be true either is true or becomes true. The fact is, within the province of the tank, whatever you believe to be true either is true or becomes true, not just in the mind. So you leave the tank in an entirely new space and new world. The language and the bodies are different, the structure of the planet and world are different, the structure of the universe itself is different. You will not necessarily come out on a planet corresponding to earth. There are many planets within a world— we should really say universe, shouldn't we? Or you could say realm, that's what the Tibetans say. Realm doesn't correspond to the language of today. The language of today would call it the universe, so don't think of it as a planet, think of it as an entire universe within which there are almost unlimited worlds. For all practical purposes, they're unlimited. Do you know what I mean by for all practical purposes?

There's a physics class, you know what physics is? A belief system based on magic except that the magic in that case happens to be nuclear. At any rate, in a physics class somebody asked,

What do you mean by for all practical purposes?

The professor said,

I want all the women to line up on that side of the room, and all the men to stand on the other side. Now, I want you to take one large step toward each other, toward the center of the room so the two lines of men and women will come one step closer on each side. Now take half that step.

So they took half that step.

Now, take half that step again.

So they took half that step.

Now, take half the step that you took just then.

So they did that and they kept going and going and

going and going until the two lines were in the center of the room but not quite together, and he said,

Now look, theoretically speaking, if you keep halfing the distance that you proceed forward, these two lines will never meet; however, you will be close enough for all practical purposes.

Okay, get back to work and get your category session and start to learn to use the tank and the sensations and the perceptions that go on in the tank in order to make your transference, and if you would like to, just take a few minutes with that and then go ahead and work with the tank again. I think it's almost time for your dinner. Maybe we won't see you again, maybe we will, so....

The Thought You Must Never Think

Did you have any trouble getting through the tank space itself? Past being in the tank, noticing that you're floating, sensing your body a lot. That's what I wanted to deal with in this talk. The reason that we had to go into the tank first is to give you the definite knowledge that the tank space is really there and that it does take a little bit to get beyond the body and beyond the tank. It's a little rough to get past that. There are two kinds of basic tank experiences that you can go for, what are called TA and ETA experiences. TA is a terrestrial activity, an activity that limits itself to the planet and the environs of the planet, and ETA is extraterrestrial activity, activity which takes you to totally different universes. There are also other things, there are intra and inter universal activities that you can go into. Basically, I want to talk to you about why you might be having trouble getting beyond the tank space. First, the tank is a new environment for your body, which means that your body has to adjust to it. You're asking the body to do a lot when you ask it to adjust to that space in a few hours. You won't genuinely use that tank beyond the material universe just with one or two tank experiences. The first tank experience is almost always connected with the tank space, being in the tank, having a body, floating in the solution, adjusting the body to the breathing, to the atmosphere and so on.

The second tank experience if you are prepared for it can be far better. You can use the tank to probably 60% or 70% of its capacity. The tank is not primarily designed just to get you out of the body or to get you out of this universe because if you get out of the body or out of the universe either accidentally or deliberately without additional knowledge, it won't do you any good. You're bound to come back in. There's a refractory point, and you will come back into it even though you escaped for a short amount of time or for a long amount of time. Eventually you will come back into it, which leads us to the question of why you're in this universe in the first place, and secondly why you're not having a good time here. By having a good time, I don't mean that you are unhappy here all the time but why you're not having as good a time as can be had, why the sense of fun is gone from the universe. Even though you occasionally get it, you do also lose it just as much.

Another basic thing that I want to cover with you in this talk is a subject which is really relatively unavailable to humans. I want to get into that subject a little bit because it'll help you get beyond the tank space and out beyond this universe, certainly out beyond your body. For that we have to understand why this universe is, why it exists. To understand that you must hear of a subject which may be entirely new to you.

When you first hear about this subject you might get the idea that the subject is so vast that it is completely unknowable, and before I even tell you what the subject is, I want to assure you that the subject is definitely an understandable and knowable subject and not as vast as it seems. It's composed of very simple parts but they form an apparently complex situation or study. You can learn basically everything you need to know about this in a matter of perhaps a few days, but then to learn to apply it requires that you practice and test out and examine all of these points — and I stress with you that you do not implicitly believe anything I say, listen to it and test it as much as is possible in the time that we have, in the workshop. I'll point out ways that you can test it and find out whether these things are true or not.

The rumor goes, there is no material universe but we get the effect of a material universe. It seems very solid, and yet we can take an individual and free him from the solidity of the universe quite simply in a matter of 10 or 15 minutes. That would not be a very nice thing to do to someone without giving them in addition the information that they need to be able to remain outside of it and to be able to consciously come back into it without being trapped in it. What you need to know in order to get past the tank space itself is the structure, construction, and cause of universes; the whole subject of universes, how they're made, how they're kept together, how they're taken apart, how one universe differs from another, and how to get from one universe to another. Perhaps hearing about that subject might make the hackles rise a little— just the idea that one could know that. I don't mean the physical laws that make up universes, I mean the laws that hold them together, the laws that create the physical laws, the chemical laws, the magnetic laws, and so on. If you understand what created a universe, what made it happen, then you understand how to take it apart.

Now, I don't know if you've ever gotten this feeling but when you're in training, when you're doing some work in this area, very often you'll get the creepy sensation that there is some thought somewhere that you're very close to but that you must not ever think. Did you ever get that idea? There's a thought that you must not think, something that you really have to keep from yourself. Whenever you get close to it there is a feeling as if something was winding up to an explosive point. You might get the shakes. You might get tingling sensations. You might even feel faint or weak or sick to your stomach. As soon as you put your attention somewhere else– and you probably do quite a bit to get your attention off this whatever it is—it goes away, it starts to subside.

That thought that you must never think, that you're avoiding, is the complete knowledge of how this universe was created, how it was made, and how it's being held together. There is the idea, you tend to get the feeling, that if you ever remember it, the universe will explode in your face. It will cease to exist, and in a way, you're quite right, but it will only cease to exist for a moment or two, and then you'll be right back in it again. Even that moment or two is pretty unbearable for most folks. The main reason, and this is something you have to discover in yourself, and it's really why you're here, that you cannot go beyond this universe into other universes is simply because you haven't yet learned to do without. You haven't learned to function without a universe, particularly without this universe. If you could learn to function without this universe then you would not be tied to it.

$$\varsigma 1 \cdot 3 \cdot 88$$

E.J. Gold, *Step Up, Step Down,*
Pen and Ink, Rives BFK, 1988.

Then you could come here and play.

The transit state or bardo state is a state of substitution. The transit state is basically a substitute for not having a universe. It's a function of the being which means that it's something you don't do deliberately. It apparently is done to you because it's a function rather than a decision or a created action on your part. When you're not in a universe you go into the transit state. If there was no place else for you to go you'd be in transit, in other words. When you go between universes you pass rapidly or slowly through the state of transit. One of the problems about moving from universe to universe is the rapidity with which it occurs. It usually occurs quite explosively, and so one of the techniques that you could pick up eventually is how to dampen that explosion or how to go through from one universe to another without the explosive experience. Very basically I can tell you that the logic behind that comes from the concept of Planck's Constant.

Now, the tank space is tied to the body space. The idea that you are in a body is reinforced by the fact that you have or believe that you have sensations from the body. Without sensations you would no longer believe that you were in a body, and without sensations you would not be tied to the body. The body would not be able to trap you without sensations, because without sensations you could very easily move your location outside a body, to another body outside the universe; to another universe and so on, it'd be quite easy for you to do. The sensations counter those actions. What else does that? All your life you've been told that you are a body, to take care of your body, to not fall with your body, to not hurt your body, to patch up your body, to feed your body, and all the while you've been told that you only go around once in life and that you are a body, no doubt about it.

If you have the good fortune, from our standpoint, to not relate well with the body, in a sense that you tend to leave it quite often, why, this society will just condemn you for that. What, you left the body? How dare you! You stay inside that thing and continue to animate it. For some reason humans do not like a body that is not animated. They don't like to see a body that doesn't have someone in it, and they also don't like to see you or feel you floating around somewhere near the body, playing puppet master with it, pulling it on strings and moving it around. They want you inside that thing just like they are, just like everyone else is. We're all stuck together here. So when you find out how to get out of that thing, you're going to run up against a great many individuals who would prefer to have you back in there and will do anything they can to do so.

If you doubt that you should read some Elizabeth Kubler-Ross accounts of people who have become clinically dead, gone out of the body, hovered above it, watched people working on it, getting it all patched up and saying come back in there. Reluctantly, because they're causing a lot of grief, they will come back into the body just to satisfy the people who are their body's companions, who are identified with being relatives of that body or friends of that body. Well, what makes those bodies in the first place? What makes these really solid objects? What makes everything here? This universe is basically not here. It does not exist. So, what holds the apparency of its existence in place? How did that happen? It happened simply because we are here, not because it is.

The basic idea is that there is a total confusion, a completely backwards idea about human beings. There's the human idea and there's the Being idea. The human idea is that we are here because the universe is. The Being knows that's

E.J. Gold, *Stepping Out*
Pen and Ink, Rives BFK, 1987.

quite wrong, and that's not why we're here at all. There's a total variance in knowledge. The human propaganda is that we are here because the universe is here. The Being knows differently. The Being realizes that the universe is here because we are. The universe is the result of the interactions between Beings. Why, if we didn't have anything to push around between ourselves we'd have absolutely no way to play with each other, and what else are we going to do with eternity? That's why the universe exists, because we do. We are here, and we're playing with each other and here we are throwing around these masses, and after a while of throwing around these masses, they begin to pile up and we begin to put less and less effort into playing with the things, and after a while the thing starts packing up solid, and that's what's happened to this universe, it has packed up solid.

Now, if you uncover the mystery of this universe, why it is, and if you backtrack it to find out how it was produced, you still are not going to be able to blow this universe out of existence because you didn't do it alone – we all did it. That's why you very often will hear that you're not going anywhere until we all go. That's why the Bodhisattvas, the Arhats and the Sufis, they don't go anywhere; the Buddha's right, no one goes anywhere until we all go. That's basically true; however, you can visit other universes and you can become free of this one, but you may not leave this universe permanently until everyone is able to leave it permanently. However, that doesn't mean you have to be continually stuck in this universe, and it doesn't mean that you have to be subject to it, a slave to it. You can discover how to use this universe, how to work with it, how to make it work for you. The basic discovery is that we are not here because the universe is here, but the universe is here because we are. If you understand that, then we've got half the problem solved. Now, let's take a look at the tank.

You go into the tank, and the tank is a functional exit and entry point to this universe. In the tank you no longer have to relate to or communicate with anyone. You are completely alone. You are free from the tank to move out of and back into the universe. The tank does not obey the same laws that this universe obeys. The tank is not created under the same laws. It violates many laws in this universe, and as you work more and more toward becoming a transit operator, you will find that these laws that are violated will be pointed out to you. You'll discover the laws that are violated and why they are violated and how they can be violated in that kind of space.

When you get into the tank you can focus on several questions, one of which is,

Who are you really apart from your identity?

You know that you are not your identity. You know that your identity limits you.

When you let go of your identity, who are you?

What creates your individuality?

Another question you could ask is,

How can you break free now from the physical limitations of the tank?

I am not here because this tank is here, this tank exists because I am here, so, obviously, all you have to do is change your concept about the tank and think of the tank in totally different categories. Think of yourself as not being in a tank. Now explain all the phenomena that you're experiencing in a completely new way. You seem to be floating, well, don't explain that with epsom salt water. Explain that in a completely different way. Suppose you're getting a sensation in your right leg. Explain that, not as a sensation in your right leg or as a sensation at all, but in a completely different way.

Find a new and completely different explanation for any phenomenon that occurs, whether it's a breathing response to the atmosphere or a drip of water from the ceiling of the tank, or a sound. Follow that out. If that's true then take a look at the rest of that universe and see what must be true about it. Follow out the logic of it until you've built an entire universe based on a different explanation of the phenomena that you're experiencing. Keep doing that until you begin to see the imagery connected with it – and you will. You will get the visual perception of that other universe. You may or may not choose to move through it, that's up to you; but at least go to a new perception of it by finding another explanation for the phenomena.

Remember also that when you're in the tank, you are in your own universe, you are not in the shared universe, and therefore anything you decide is true or becomes true as you decide it more and more. The more certainly you decide the more true it becomes. You can create an entire universe within that space and as you create it pay attention to how you're creating it, and you will learn how this universe is created. If you do it really well you will not know whether this universe was created through the tank coming this way or whether you went the other way. You won't know. You leave the tank, and you don't know whether you're leaving the tank or not by that point; you may still be in the tank for all you know. In fact you might be in the tank right now. I talked with one individual who's been using the tank for several years, and I asked him whether he had ever gotten past the tank space and he said,

I used to have a lot of trouble and I never could figure

it out. I would have a terrible time in the tank. I'd be in the tank, and be in the tank and be in the tank, and then I'd get out of the tank, and go about my daily business, and then go back to the tank and try to get out through the tank again and it took a long time before I realized that I was in the tank all the time and that I had very definitely succeeded in creating a universe. The thing that happened was that I thought that it was created the other way around, that you created a totally different universe, so, what I find myself doing is creating the same universe over and over again.

This bewildered voyager finally discovered that his native state, his real condition, his everyday existence, is to be in the tank, and when he goes past the tank space he moves out of the tank, not by floating but by sitting up and opening and closing the tank doors behind him; going out of the tank, going in to take a shower, getting dressed and going out into the world. He finally discovered that that is what he is creating and that the tank itself is real and every so often, either every other day or every day, sometimes after only three or four hundred lifetimes or a thousand lifetimes, he'll return to the tank, his real daily existence. He'll snap back to the tank and then move out from it again. So he thought that the human world was his center and that he was moving out into the tank which was somewhere outside the human world and that he was going somewhere entirely different.

You can get a better concept of the experience by realizing that the tank is genuinely your center, that you're going home when you go into the tank. You're losing your imagery, you're ceasing to create a universe. You move into the tank and you think of another universe. You sit up, open the doors and go out into that universe, and if it's the same universe as it is now for you, and it continues to be the same

E.J. Gold, *Off the Wall*
Pen and Ink, Rives BFK, 1987.

universe, you had better take a look at yourself, at your ability to move beyond the limits that you've set up for yourself.

Again the constant concept of the tank is backwards just as if you ask a human why this is all happening, the human will say, with human consciousness,

We're here because this universe is here and we grew up in it. We appeared here in this universe because this universe is here and we are part of it.

If you ask an individual who's gone beyond human consciousness they will say,

No, that isn't true, the universe is here because we are.

Well, the tank is the same thing; if you ask a human what the tank is or what they imagine the tank to be, someone with human consciousness will say,

You go into the tank and while you're there you dream up another universe and you go there or you see it. Then you come back to the tank and you go out and you leave and you come back into this, you go out of the tank and take a shower and so on and return to this world.

The only reason it seems that way is because of one's attachment to the Human World. One cannot dream up or conceive of a world other than the Human World. As a result one becomes stuck with the Human World itself. Anyway, it's backwards. You don't leave the Human World and go through the tank into another world. You leave the Human World and go back to the tank, back to the mother. I don't mean the womb either — you go back to the mother, to the matrix of space, and you'll find that the tank's proportions are such that it becomes the matrix of space, it's built to exact proportions, the same kind of knowlege that went into building the Great Pyramid, the same proportional structures are used.

So, you return to the tank, your native state and given

E.J. Gold, *After Dinner Nap*,
Pen and Ink, Rives BFK, 1987.

that you are able to let go of the body and let go of the body sensations and given that you are able to think in entirely new categories and to conceive in entirely new categories, to have a new conception, new thought, new sensation, new perception, when you recenter in the tank you take apart the material universe as it has been and you simply reassemble it, take the basic components and reassemble them in whatever form you would like. However, if you are completely attached to the human existence and to the human world then you will, in all probability, go into the tank, lie down and have a nice bath, sit up, leave the tank and walk out once again into what you have created again, the usual.

Is it any wonder that that happens to you every time you go into the between lives area, everytime you die to this world? That's why the tank is a practice at death, that's why the tank is so connected with transit, because you have a chance to die before you die and the whole point is practice and the next point is knowing how to create, how to put it together, how to reassemble it in a different way, how to think in new categories, how to free yourself from the constant limitation to which you've subjected yourself: the limitation of being human. So, if you go into the tank and you then come back out of the tank and you're in the human world once again—you had better take a look at your own programming, at your own limits, at your own structure of being, what you do. Coming back out of the tank, you should be able to fashion anything that you want to, and yet you fashion only what you're used to, only what you're familiar with, only what is predictable for you, and eminently and inevitably predictable for you. I can give very good odds that you're going to come out of there with two arms, two legs, and only one head. I can give you very good odds, excellent odds, that you're going to be speaking human language. I can give you very good odds that you will be visually perceiving through your eyes again, as usual.

There are a couple of things I want you to find out for yourself, like, how can this universe exist for everyone else, and you leave it and go off into another universe? When you leave the tank you come out into a totally different universe, and yet the people seem similar to the ones that were in the other universe. And how can all universes exist simultaneously within the same point, within the structural sphere? How is it that everyone has a corresponding entity into which they inevitably move if they do change universes, so, no matter what universe you emerge in there is someone corresponding to someone that you know in the other universe or in an other universe? These are things that I want you to look at and find out about.

You also will not be able to move out of the Human World until you find out what's holding you here, what's keeping you here; why you keep creating it, why you keep making that one, even though you have a chance to do something else. You go into the tank. The tank, I assure you, is your native state. I can assure you absolutely that it is your native state, that you are not going into a tank at all, that you only see it that way because your psyche demands it. But in fact you are absolutely not going into a tank, and we are absolutely not having a weekend workshop and I am absolutely not what I seem to be. The point is, when you have a chance to do something else why do you do the same thing? When an opportunity presents, why do you continue to do the same thing? Why do you keep emerging in the human world? That, unfortunately is not the subject of a weekend workshop.

Basically the key for you today in working with the

tank, with the native state, is that when you go into the native
state, begin to find new explanations for what is happening,
for your perceptions, for sounds, thoughts, concepts, that
occur. Find a totally new explanation for that. Continue
finding new explanations. Don't allow the old explanations
for these things to satisfy you. Don't be satisfied with the
usual explanations. Find a totally new one for everything that
happens. While as a result of that, if you go into a paranoid
state, don't worry about it, find a new explanation for that,
and so on. I want you to find new explanations for everything
and play with the idea that there is a different explanation
other than the explanation with which you're familiar and
don't worry about it. If you want to we can always go back to
the old explanation, if you want to guide yourself back to the
human world where all your friends are.

I mean you might end up in another world and not
have any work, might not have a job, no place to stay, you're
walking around naked. Can you imagine yourself emerging
completely naked on a completely strange world, a world
where you don't speak the language, you have no money or
whatever passes for money, you have no job, you have no-
where to live, you don't know what the environment is going
to be like? You have no idea what the conditions of the environment are—maybe it's terribly cold, maybe it's terribly
warm, you don't know even what season you're in at the
moment—you just walk out, you have no idea what season
you're in relative to other seasons if there are any.

You don't know what the rules of conduct are, you
don't know what the culture demands of you, you might just
break a taboo that calls for the death penalty by simply spit-
ting on the sidewalk or something. You don't know, and here
you are naked walking down the street in a totally alien city,

E.J. Gold, Limbo Rock,
Pen and Ink, Rives, BFK, 1988

on a totally alien planet, and you suddenly feel the urge to take a crap. Now, where are you going to go?

Suppose that you don't even know that there might be seven sexes there, and you see a bathroom and you walk in and it turns out to be the equivalent of the wrong bathroom. You walk into a bathroom for the seventh sex and here you are the third sex and they bust you for indecent exposure or something.

Or you look down and you say, my god, I'm naked. I've got to get some clothes. Oh, let's say you discover somehow that clothing is free, and so you go into a clothing store and you ask for some clothing and you put it on and you walk out into the street. It turns out that you can only wear clothing in the privacy of your own home, and it is completely taboo to wear clothing in public.

You have no idea of what the rules of behavior are. You can't read the street signs. You don't know whether it says walk or don't walk. You know, green might mean stop and red might mean go. It might not even be those colors. It might be totally alien colors. How do you function in that kind of a space? Well, naturally, you keep coming back to earth, coming back to the Human World. Of course you do. You know the laws, you know the rules, you know the language, you know the people, you have work here, you have a place to stay, it's no risk. ... So, until you're capable of handling that kind of situation where there is high risk, the chances are very good that you are going to come back to the Human World or something like it.

One of the things you could do, is you could learn some of the cultural differences between the Human World and other possible universes that you could go and visit. If you learn those things then you wouldn't feel badly about

E.J.Gold, *I'll Be Right Up*,
Pen and Ink, Rives BFK, 1987.

leaving the Human World. That's one of the things that is accomplished on a long term basis in a thing called a School. You learn the behavioral things, and you learn the cultural differences between the worlds so you're able to leave the human world and go out into another world or other worlds. You learn the language, the customs, and so on. You might even, before you leave the human world and go into another world, arrange for employment and a place to stay. This is possible. I'm not telling you something that is totally far out or a fantasy. I'm telling you something that is absolutely and demonstrably possible for you.

There are 329 worlds that are close enough to the Human World to pass. There'll only be a few differences. It's demonstrable that you could end up in one of those worlds and work through that and notice the differences that occur and then re-enter through the tank and come back to the one you started in. The reason to come back to the one you started in is because you have a connection with the school. The school exists, however, in all worlds; in all possible worlds, the school exists. Why does the school exist? Because the school is connected with the tank, whatever you're calling the tank currently. In other words, the school is that which surrounds the gateway to the native state. So, you can consider that there is no such thing as a school. In the Human World, it's called a school. In the Hell World, it's called a gatekeeper. In the Brute World, it's called a gambling casino.

The gambling casino invariably surrounds the gateway. It isn't really a gambling casino but it seems that way, because there is gaming. Actually, it's called the gaming room. The human equivalent is a gambling casino and so it goes. In every single world there is a gateway and there is, surrounding that gateway, the apparency of something or other that prepares you as a traveller. You could think of it as an inn or a hotel just outside the gateway for those who are going into the gate and then back out into another world. It serves the purpose of a waystation for someone coming into this world from another world. In fact, in the world of Jealous Gods, that's what it's called, is the waystation. It's called *swetta*. That may help you some day, don't forget that word. If you ask for *swetta*, you know what that means.

There are some individuals who can pass consciously from one world to another. They are conscious travellers. Those individuals come here, spend an afternoon perhaps, have a meal, go through the tank and emerge in another world, and they may not return here for some time. Other individuals are just learning how to do this. Other individuals don't even dream of its possibility and would laugh like hell if you ever mentioned it. Other individuals believe it's complete fantasy. The only time they wouldn't believe it's complete fantasy is if they saw somebody get into the tank and not come out, but they won't get that far because they'll freak out before they get there. They'll freak out at the waystation but that does occur. The only time you know for sure that it really occurs is when you yourself make the journey.

Okay, so far, you've gone into the waystation. Here you are at the waystation, and I'm the innkeeper here, and I really am the inn keeper of the waystation of the human world. I also happen to be the innkeeper of the others, but how that works is something that I want you to find out, because I'm looking for replacements and, well, we all do a gig at this, each one of us in our turn does a gig at this. Every traveller has a turn at being the operator, the waystation operator. Precisely how that goes on you are welcome to discover. The point is, here we are at the waystation.

Okay, now you go to the gate that this waystation keeps, and you get to the gate, and you stand right underneath the gate, right in the center of the gate, and then with all possibilities before you, you turn around and come back the way you came. That's why I'm not too surprised to see you, and so, we'll try again.

Don't Linger in the Doorway

Here one is in a state which we could characterize as reverie. In reverie one can travel with one's consciousness. One can visualize quite deeply. In the state of reverie one is able to transcend the barriers of the external reality and go into one's own reality. In Delta two, Delta three and Delta four there are various stages of sleep. Tonight we'll get into Delta two state with Delta three and four. Delta one, the reverie state, is going to be very important to you; Delta three and four are going to be important to know about. Delta three is the dream state. Delta two is the famous R.E.M. state, that is, Rapid Eye Movements. And Delta four is a blackout state.

Delta four can be entered into only briefly. It is a very fast state, and one does not remain in the Delta four state for very long periods of time. Delta four is in fact nothing more than a portal to the Delta three. The Delta three state, the

dream state, has a safety factor, a valve; you must go down to
Delta four and return to Delta three in order to arrive in Delta
three. In order to leave the dream state one cannot go directly
into Delta two. One must go back through Delta four and
back up into Delta two and one, so, Delta four is a safety
factor to insure that you will not enter or leave the dream state
directly into Delta two.

There is a very definite cut off between the dream state
and the ordinary waking consciousness. In other words,
through the Delta four state one cannot normally retain
memory of what has gone on in the dream state and during
the dream state one does not have contact with the Beta or
ordinary consciousness. I'll show you how and why this
works and why you need this in ordinary consciousness, how
it protects ordinary consciousness, in a moment.

So, we have two things to discuss: one is the reason for
the Delta four state and the other is the use of the Delta one
state, but I want to show you where the other states are in
relation to one another. As we go up the scale through Delta
two and Delta one, we find a state just above Delta one which
is called the Theta state. The Theta state in biofeedback
technology simply means a state of meditation. So, we could
say that the Theta state is the meditative state. Above the
Theta state is the Alpha, a state of light meditation. It is also
a state of non thought. One has a pure perception of the
environment, one has a pure perception of Self and if one has
done other work in addition to these states, one has a direct
perception of one's feelings, sensations, and knowledge.
Above the Alpha state is the Beta state or ordinary waking
conciousness.

In hertz, in case you'd like this for notes, the Beta state
runs 13-35, the Alpha state runs about 8-12 and the Theta

E.J. Gold, *Ninth Month*
Pen and Ink, Rives BFK, 1987.

state runs about 3 -7, and the Delta states run 3 and below, down to unmeasurable. Okay, these are in Hertz. Hertz is the name for the frequency. They used to be called cycles per second. Now they're called Hertz, so, 3 cycles per second, 7 cycles per second, 8 -12 cycles per second, 13 -35 cycles per second. Biofeedback technologists believe that these things have to do with something or other about wave theory and also with the generation of impulses in the brain. However, they have more to do with sound than they do with systemic responses of the brain and nervous system, particularly the autonomic, in which everyone today is very interested.

The Beta state is ordinary waking conciousness. Normally, this is the state which dominates even though all of these waves and states are going on at the same time. When we say that someone is in Beta, we mean that there is a measurable dominance of the Beta wave as opposed to the other waves. It is larger and heavier. If we cut some of the Beta waves, some of the roof brain activity which is the constant chatter that goes on in your head, the constant images that keep coming up, the continual running on in your head, other wave lengths will become dominant. The first that becomes dominant generally is the Alpha. The Alpha tends to dominate the Theta just as the Beta tends to dominate the Alpha. Theta dominates the Delta, so as we cut the Beta, the roof brain, we are in the Alpha state. As we cut the Alpha state we are in the Theta state. As we cut the Theta state, even deeper than meditation, we are in a state of reverie. We don't want to cut reverie and REM and the dream state down to a blackout, do we? We're going to not use Delta two through four. I wanted you to know what they were because I want you to be able to avoid them.

We're going to work with the Delta one state, the state

of reverie. This is the state in which one is able to contact the transit experience and this is not just the experience between lives, this is the experience which one has anywhere outside the universe. The Delta one state is one of the few things that is, in terms of consciousness, controllable. The Delta four simply is a gateway, a protective mechanism to isolate the ordinary waking consciousness from the dream consciousness. If one wishes to probe into the dream state one must break through the Delta four state with one's sense of consciousness, one's thread of consciousness. That is the subject for an entire course. It is possible but it is not wise. Some individuals have gone into that realm of exploration, and some individuals have come back from it, and some have not. So, we don't want to touch that, and none of the things which you will be doing at this time will be anywhere near probing into the Delta four state. There's absolutely no danger involved with the states that you will be working with.

I want to mention that there is a tremendous margin of safety; the tank is a safe space and so is the use of the tank. In tens of thousands of experiments with the tank there has not, to date, been one negative experience. I don't mean that people haven't gotten into fear spaces or whatever, but there has not been an accident with the tank and there is not likely to be.

But let's look at the state of reverie. The state of reverie is basically a travelling consciousness. It's a consciousness which can enter and leave the material universe. It's a consciousness which is not bound by the material universe. It is therefore, basically, a limitless consciousness.

We're going to use the state of reverie to go after the transit experience. We can do it, it is demonstrable, it is simple and it is easy. You will get the transit experience if you

E.J. Gold, *Typing in the Sky,*
Pen and Ink, Rives BFK, 1987.

follow directions. It's really mapped out, and in connection with that I want to point out something to you about working with states, not using any method. It takes an enormous amount of energy pumped into three nervous systems, three entirely separate nervous systems, in order to bring about a full and conscious exit from the body . The amount of energy that is required for this trip is equivalent to digging ten ditches if they were fifty feet long and two feet deep, two feet wide. Most of the work that you are going to be doing here this weekend will be learning how to develop this energy and in the tank, learning how to apply it.

The tank, like any other powerful method, requires from you a definite price. It requires the price of a certain amount of energy. Under ordinary circumstances you do not have that energy to pay and therefore the techniques for getting that energy will be given to you during this workshop. Some techniques for applying this energy will be given to you also during this workshop but where you go and what you do there is entirely your own business. There will be some guide-lines which you may choose to follow or you may not, it 's up to you. It is your consciousness. It is your life.

What we're hoping to do is open the door as wide as you would like it to open so that you can see as much as you would like to see in the hope that perhaps you will go a little farther this time than you went last time. And also in the hope that you will go farther than that next time and even farther than that the time after. We tend to forget as we get closed into a limited consciousness what we really are, what we really can do, how we really relate and who we are to each other. The tank experience will certainly bring these back into your life because it forms the bridge between higher con-sciousness and human consciousness.

I wanted to say a few words more in relation to exercise and what it has to do with the tank. Many people do not realize that if the body can be developed, so can the mind. But surely you've seen that people can build incredible bodies and people can become very, very powerful, very strong, physically. Did anyone watch the Olympics, the summer Olympics? Wasn't that marvelous? People can train themselves to be faster, to leap higher, to run faster, to swim faster, to be more graceful, to lift heavier weights than anybody has ever done. All kinds of things. If you ask what the purpose is behind it, well, the purpose really isn't to throw a javelin so many feet or meters, it really is not to break the record on the hundred meter, it isn't to swim faster than anyone has ever accomplished before then, those are symptoms of the purpose.

The purpose is to use as much of the body as is humanly possible. It's very often bandied about that we only use ten percent of the available functions of the brain. Very few individuals realize that this is also true of the body. The body is used also to perhaps one tenth its capacity and one must then make the realization that this is also true of the emotions; there is a separate, emotional something or other which is similar to the mind as it handles, produces, creates, contacts, puts together and analyzes thought. And the body which does the same with action, objects and the environment, the relationship of the body with the environment and the body's internal control system, life support system of the body and there is equally an emotional, if you like, brain.

One can see quite easily that the body can be trained and that one can become quite able, quite strong, quite competent with the body. The body can be extended past all limits that are experienced by ordinary humanity. In short there are some people who can use their bodies far better than anyone else can. It also goes without saying, not that it shouldn't be said, that there are some individuals that can use their emotions better and more strongly, more powerfully, if you wish, and more ably than others. It also goes without saying, but it should be said that there are some individuals who use their minds with much greater power and much greater ability than many others.

It has long been a myth in the western world that someone who has a powerful mind just happens to have a powerful mind and did nothing whatever to bring that about. What are some of the characteristics of a powerful mind? Perhaps this might help you to visualize, to get an image of what I'm talking about, if I point out some of the things that a powerful mind can do. A powerful mind is capable of dealing with the environment as it is without altering it. It is capable of dealing with others by seeing them as they are and by not putting any demands on them to be some other way. A powerful mind is able to get things accomplished without running over someone else's purpose, without interfering with someone else's aims or goals. The powerful minds that you've heard about are called miracle makers, the mysterious lamas, the mystics, people of whom it's been said that they floated through the air or walked through walls or produced solid objects from thin air. There's no reason why not.

An interesting byline to that is that the mind is definitely superior to the body. The mind definitely controls and operates the body. Everything that's happening with the body is something that's directed by the mind. The mind also directs and controls emotions, even though most humans would prefer not to think that. Perhaps you like to think of your emotions as something more organic than something which is directly controlled or created, and yet emotions are decided upon and created within you by the mind quite automatically. The point I'm making is that the mind can be exercised, and through exercise it can be developed.

Now, look at what we are talking about. We're talking about parts of the human being: the body, the emotions, and the mind. All of those parts of the human being can be developed through exercise, in the same way that the body can be developed. Now this may be a surprise to you. Has it ever occured to you, if those things are possible, that the spirit can also be developed through exercise, the spiritual consciousness? If you realize that, then you have made the correct decision to go on with this work. You know why you're here. You know what you hope to accomplish, and you at least have an idea of how to go about it because all of these things are true.

Now, I would like to call your attention to the tank itself. If you think of the tank as a space, and you go into tank space and you explore tank space, and you are into the tank, you will be going into a dead end. It's like trying to go through a door, opening the door and standing in the doorway, if you get hung-up in tank space. I want to warn you that it does happen. It perhaps will happen the first time, maybe for a short while. It depends upon your ability to let go of the body. The tank essentially is a doorway. Do not stop there. Do not linger in the tank space, go on through. Many times one will not go through the tank space to the other side because one is concerned that return might become impossible. Return will not become impossible.

You will discover that on the other side there are guides whom you will recognize and they will bring you out and they will bring you back and then you come through the

E.J. Gold, *Squared Off*
Pen and Ink, Rives BFK, 1987.

tank once again and into this universe. You can think of the
tank itself as an entry and exit point into and out of the material universe. You can think of it as an entry and exit point into
your deep self, your inner states of consciousness. You can
think of the guides as personal, impersonal, cosmic or
psychological, as you wish. You'll be shown how to get into
and out of the tank, how to use the tank itself. The staff mem-
bers will show you that. The primary point is to gather the
energy, to bring the energy in, to bring your nervous system to
a peak capacity and go into the tank and let it go, let it rip. In
connection with doing that your guides here, the staff, will
show you the exercises to do, and we'll build the nervous
system strength.

At the peak point you will be given your first tank
session; after that point you will again build the energy structure and then once again go in the tank. We will repeat this as
often as it is possible given the number of people in the intensive and given the amount of energy that can be rebuilt in a
short time. The faster you accumulate and build the energy
necessary for a tank trip, the more tank experience you'll be
able to have. I want to caution you however that quantity
alone does not constitute a good workshop, particularly with
the tank. It is how far out you go with it, how you work with
and relate to what you are shown. It primarily is not what you
experience while you are there but what you bring back with
you. Are there any questions before we complete this orientation? Is there anything you need to know?

There are a couple of things I'd like to mention. One is
that the diet is extremely important. It is a special diet. Please,
do not break it. It is a diet that is designed to give you the
most possible energy. As I say, we are working with three
different nervous systems, the sympathetic, autonomic, and

central nervous systems.

Another extremely important thing is to not do any other practices such as pranayama or yoga during this intensive, because it does take energy to do these exercises. You will be given exercises to do, and those exercises will be designed to raise rather than expend energy. Another important thing is to not indulge in talking and chatter. Study, rest, allow the energy to build. Don't throw the energy away through the mouth. It's extremely important.

You're going to do a reading first that'll be the introduction, and I'll tell you what you're in for with this. You'll be reading the introduction to *The American Book of the Dead*. That will be a very valuable experience in terms of this, and this will orient you in terms of the area in Delta one, in the reverie state, that you are looking for, and it will orient you in terms of where you're looking to travel. There are two kinds of tank experiences, one of which is verbal and the other is non-verbal. You are going to take both kinds of tank trips. Your first tank trip will be non-verbal. After the tank experience you'll be given tank report forms, and you will write out in detail what occured during the tank experience, after your shower.

Who has used the tank before? Okay, for those of you who haven't used the tank before, let me explain a few things about the tank. The first thing is, you must never let go in the tank, by that I mean, do not wee-wee in the tank. The reason for that is, although the tank solution is completely sterile it still makes a funny odor, and it makes it hard to live with. There is a bathroom right in the tank room so you just get up out of the tank and go to the bathroom and then return to the tank; it won't cause you a lot of difficulty. It follows without saying that you obviously don't relieve yourself in any way in the tank. You shower before you go into the tank and you shower absolutely thoroughly. You give yourself a good shampoo. You must do this to get the oils off the body. You're going into a supersaturated solution of magnesium sulfate. $MgSO_4$ — Epsom salts. It is a much more buoyant solution than ordinary salt water, but it needs to be kept clean. Therefore, we shower before we go into the tank and we shower when we leave the tank to wash the salts off.

Another thing is, if you haven't brought a comb, then we'll arrange for it. You brush your hair out so that loose hairs don't get into the tank. Do not go into the tank after you have eaten because you'll be too logey. You'll tend to fall asleep. Although the meals are very high quality they are not large quantity and the reason for that again is that you don't become logey and fall out during the tank experience. You want to remain in exactly the state that you want, Delta one. You do not want to go any deeper than that. You will not be having tank experiences during your ordinary sleeping hours. If anyone sleeps during the day and works at night, does swing shift or graveyard shift, let us know and we will arrange it so that you will have your tank experience during your ordinary waking hours.

Oh, there's a temperature control system and a small computer on top of the tank, please don't touch that. The temperature is controlled to a hundreth of a degree and it must remain exactly at that temperature; otherwise an individual can go into a comatose condition. If the temperature is too high or if the temperature is too low, it is too uncomfortable and the tank experience does not occur.

I really would appreciate it if the staff could say, just briefly, anything that you have found about the initial tank experience that could help somebody avoid getting hung up in the tank space.

Yeah, keep your mouth closed. Don't drink the water. It'll stay in your mouth for the hour.

Okay, anything else?

Well, don't make an effort to keep your mouth closed though. I didn't mean to keep it absolutely closed but a lot of people when they go swimming don't mind if they have water in their mouth.

Anything else?

You have to center yourself exactly in the middle because if you push gently off one side and you think that's going to get you up in the middle, about 10 minutes later you'll bump your head. Not hard. If you move extremely slowly through this, however, you will tend to center, if you just let it happen, just let yourself drift into the center.

Any other comments?

Yeah, I've got one comment about a general attitude concerning being in the tank, particularly in the early times that one goes in, which is that the tank is primarily an active experience.

You're going in to learn to acquire some abilities to do some things, and if you go in with that attitude you're much more liable to use your time in there beneficially than just space out or black out. So take the attitude that this reverie condition has an element of action or active approach toward it. I don't mean to go into a chattery kind of space but that you're going in to do something.

If anything could be said about this weekend it's that you have come here to learn to do something for yourself, not for us to do something for you, not to have something done to you, not to receive something but to learn how to do it. And once you know how to do it, you don't need a tank. The tank has become something which is, was at one time a tool, and then became a limit in itself, and then finally the limit is transcended through to another kind of experience. The point is, you came here to learn something. It's here to learn, it's available for you, go and get it. Be aggressive in that sense. I don't mean to be negatively aggressive but be aggressive in that sense, go and get it, work for it, make it happen, use it, learn to do for yourself.

Also, if they have the time set aside for an hour or two for you to go into the tank and you go in the tank and you want to get out in five minutes, it's quite fine to do that. As long as you want to go in the tank you can go in for that amount of time. It's extremely important that you understand that you are not forced to remain in the tank for a certain amount of time. There is an outside limit because other people are going to be using the tank too, but the inside limit, there is none. You can stay in the tank for 1 minute, 5 minutes, 20 minutes, 30 minutes, 45 minutes, 50 minutes, anytime before an hour. You'll be doing these in one hour trips, one hour sessions.

Inside the tank the atmosphere is different and you have to adjust to the atmosphere to breathe comfortably. The key is just to relax. If you work hard at breathing it tends to be a little loud or distracting. The main thing is just to relax and let your breathing harmonize itself to that environment and it will.

If you've been near the ocean, if you've hung out in salt water you'll be used to this.

Always Ask, "Where Am I?"

If you emerge from the tank in a completely different world, don't worry about it, because at the waystation in that world you will be taught everything. You will emerge naked and you will be taught everything you need to know. Your mind also will do something wonderful for you. What will your mind do for you if you find yourself in a completely alien space, or a totally different world? The only thing that will change for you will be the characterization of the experience. The quality of your life will be different but to you, you still emerge in the Human World until you get past human consciousness. For all you know now, you might have emerged in the God World, or you might have emerged in the Hell World.

You started out in the Human World. Can you say absolutely where you are now? It would be a good idea to put a sign outside the tank that says, "You are now entering the. . .", and it says underneath which world it is. Welcome to the Human World, welcome to the God World, welcome to the Jealous Gods, and so on. You go into the tank and you come out of the tank, and you know from the sign exactly what world you emerged in, so you say oops, get back in, and come out again until you get the right one. That's the one, the department store, second floor. It's a marvelous idea.

On the other hand, if you did that and you saw the sign out there and it said "Human World" and you went into the tank and you came back out and now it says, "Welcome to the Jealous God World," well you know ding-dongs, somebody came into the tank room and changed the sign. The only way you'd be able to tell the difference between one world and another is the quality of that world, what's happening in it. So, when you leave here this weekend, if you walk out into the Human World again it will have the same quality to it. It'll have the same old lack of communication, lack of relating, the same problems with people and with the environment, and so on, that you had before, and the chances are that you will actually, at the end of this workshop emerge once again in the Human World. You won't disappear. On the other hand, aren't there fewer of you now than there were?

I have to explain that because there is someone missing, isn't there suddenly? Two are missing? Jose went to Puerto Rico, and Wayne is still in the tank. He'll be emerging right here, that's where he's coming back. Jose had to leave and catch a plane to Puerto Rico and Fred drove him down to do that, so, that's why he's not in the group, not because he went into the tank and went into another world. I want to explain that so you don't think I'm misleading you about it. Also, there is no trap door in the tank. I want to be quite

E.J.Gold, *Jittery Walls,*
Pen and Ink, Rives BFK, 1987.

definite about that, and I want you to check it out.

However, you will discover at one point or another that you'll go into the tank, have a nice bath, and without even half-realizing it you'll be starting to think in other categories, thinking completely new concepts and you'll emerge from the tank and something will be quite radically different. Don't do anything strange. If this should occur to you now, don't worry about it. Just come out of the tank and act as if something had happened, by that I mean, tell whoever is there,

"Hey, I. . . . "

Now before I get into what to say and what to do if you do end up in an alien world, alien to you of course, is that habits are the one thing about you that never changes, unless you consciously change them. To consciously change habits takes effort and a great deal of time, lots and lots of time. It took millions and billions and trillions of years in space and time to create the habits, to accumulate unconsciously the habits you have now. It's going to take you years to substitute conscious habits, habits which will get you past the point of unconsciousness, to counteract those unconsciously accumulated habits. If you strip down your ego, your identity, your knowledge, your mind, your emotions, your concepts, your perception — you take all of that away, what is left is what is called the body of habits. I pointed this out in *The American Book of the Dead* , but I did not go into specifics about it because it's not really meant for a public dissertation. Only if you're interested at all is it possible to go further.

What you are then, your real identity, is composed of nothing more than your habits plus you as a Being which has no habits. What you are is what you have become rather than what you are. Why you do what you do, why you think what you think, why you go where you go, why you create what

E.J. Gold, *Odalisque Plumber*,
Pen and Ink, Rives BFK, 1987.

you create, why you have the concepts you have, why you have the thoughts that you have, why you have the emotions you have, why you have the friends you have, why you have the relationships and the type of relationships you have, why you take certain actions, why you make decisions the way you make them, why you have the psyche you have, why you have the personality you have—all is a result of your habits because your mind, your psyche, your body, your emotional body, all take on the characteristics of you as a Being and the habits you've accumulated.

As soon as you get into a body you indelibly print, you imprint your habits into the nervous system, the moment you enter a body. That is why you do what you do. That is why you are what you are, or why you seem to be what you seem to be, and that certainly is why you understand what you understand, you conceive of what you conceive of, and so on. All of these things relate to your habits. At some point we're going to learn to consciously substitute real habits, good ones, habits that will bring about conscious life, for the habits which have accumulated unconsciously over trillions of years and more.

That's a little side track that I wanted to take for a moment. Now, I want to tell you about getting out of the tank. When you get out of the tank, the first thing you should ask is, "Where am I?" Even if the person seems familiar, because your mind will substitute familiar images for the most alien possible images. Here is a Being and there you are as a Being. You're used to the imagery of the Human World. Your mind, in order to protect your psyche, will substitute familiar images for those images that you are actually perceiving. It won't do that for very long but it will do that for a while. When entering a completely new world you can expect that to not completely come off for two to three weeks.

   After two or three weeks you will slowly begin to break down those images that are familiar, and you will begin to perceive the world that you're in as it is. It will happen at a rather slow rate, a rate that you could take. Your mind protects you in that way.

   At first it will seem familiar, even if there's some incredibly gunky figure out there that says something like: "Oh, good-evening, I'm so glad you've come out of the tank."

   You'll hear: "Hey, how ya doin?", and you'll see somebody like Hakim standing there with a friendly grin instead of the big toothy smile on somebody that is about to send you off to the slave pits.

   Always ask, "Where am I?", when you come out of the tank.

   John Lilly doesn't do that. He says, "Father took the shoe bench out, meet me by the lawn." But he gets to say that. That immediately orients him in space, but that's a trick he's learned to do for himself. He doesn't have to ask anyone where he is, but again he's been working at going in and out, consciously travelling from one universe to another, for some forty odd years, human time, and that's just lately. So don't be embarrassed to ask that.

   There will be a guide present somewhere at the waystation, and you definitely should ask, "Where am I?", and establish that. If it's some place that you would rather not be, then definitely re-enter the tank.

   Say "I'm going back into the tank, wrong stop."

   And they'll tell you, "Fine, go ahead."

   I want to point out something else to you which is that that gateway is always open, continually open. It's always available, and you'll find it in every world, as I said. There are individuals walking around who have forgotten about that gateway, and yet every single individual in this world came through that gateway. And every individual uses that gateway at least twice in a lifetime: once at the beginning and once at the end. The idea is to get them to use it more often than that.

The problem is that the gateway very often has to be moved because individuals in the worlds hear about its existence and understand what it is. It represents a threat, either a threat of invasion or a threat of depopulation. In at least three of the major worlds, of which there are several hundred variations, or slight variations, the authorities don't like to hear that the gateway is there, because where are they going to get folks to run their machines if everybody leaves? And in those same three basic worlds they don't like to hear about the existence of a gateway because it means that invaders could come through there and take over. These are both equally valid concepts from those particular consciousnesses.

The point is that you first find out whether an individual is interested in a gateway at all, if they understand what it means, and you should qualify them to the point where you discover whether or not they already know about such gateways, know the uses of them and so on. If they do, then they don't have to be told about it, they'll find it. If they have simply forgotten about it but are interested in it, tell them where it is. If they're not interested in it but are curious about it, don't tell them about it, don't tell them where it is. When they do want to know where it is, they'll ask more questions. I don't think this is a subject for this workshop, but at some point we definitely should drill on the various forms of the waystation — who is there, who operates it, what their names are, what to say, some of the basic rules of each of the societies and so on, and to give you some places to move out into.

E.J. Gold, *Moonman,*
Pen and Ink, Rives BFK, 1987.

In the meantime, I'd like you to try, without making any effort to do it, simply to move out into something in another category, whatever category you can think of. I don't want to suggest one to you. If you end up in a different world, there'll be someone there when you leave the tank, so when you get out of the tank ask, "Where am I?" Even if it feels familiar to you, even if it looks exactly the same to you, examine whether or not you're projecting onto that your familiar images. Try to see it as it is.

Now, if you're very straight with yourself, it's possible for you to leave this world today and emerge in a completely different world and see it as it is without the human image on it. That is possible, and it has happened. If that happens for you that's great, that's exactly what we're looking for. If it doesn't happen that way don't worry about it. Ask where you are if you're not in the Human World, and the guide will be absolutely straight with you. They'll tell you exactly where you are, there's no reason for them not to. If you're not in the Human World go back into the tank until the Human World does again appear, until you can logic it back together, and emerge once again in the Human World.

The reason for that is because that is your place now in the work, in terms of working on yourself. You need more data before you begin to move around through the worlds and to find you a place in another world at this point would not really be very good. You'd have to re-establish your whole survival level all over again. It takes so much time that you'd waste a tremendous amount of time in doing that. You can't really re-establish all your survival lines and expect to have time to work on yourself and to get the information you need in order to become a conscious inter-world traveller. Okay, I'm going to send you back down there and see what happens.

If you make this one again, fine; if you make another one, fine; either way you'll at least get experience with your native state in the tank.

Incidentally, there is one more thing.

Don't think of the tank as something that is not you. Try to assume the shape of the tank as you're in it and think in totally different categories. Explain everything that happens completely differently, as far differently as you can.

At first, when a drop of water happens, a drop of water, a drop of water. No, that was the human consciousness that used to think that. What that really is..., and go ahead and explain it. It might take you a while to explain it in a different way. Don't worry about it, let the lag occur.

Are there any questions about anything?

If there are no questions, I have no answers. Now then what was your question?

I was informed that in order for real change to occur it's necessary to sense, look, and listen.

In answer to your question, no there is no such thing as an interruption to anything. (At this point a child had entered the room and made noise. The speaker exhibited annoyance before speaking.) It may be your idea that something is happening in a straight line, but no, that is not true. And if you want to sense, look, and listen, if that's what you have to do in order to have real change, you go ahead, if you feel that that's what'll do it.

I understand that you have to be present, have to be in present time. You have to be in present time and present space in order to learn anything of real value. That was made as an authoritative statement, a true, objective statement and I was wondering about its truth.

What were you wondering about its truth?

Do you think that will do you any good? Let me ask you this. Can you change a habit by acting yesterday? You are your habits. Can you see that? Can you see that everything else in you dies?

Can you see that everything else about you dies: your consciousness, your intellect, your emotions, your body. Under ordinary death those things are not translated with you. Of course at the completion point, they become something else, they enter into a transition state and by being a counterpart to the self, they become permanently fixed, you get that?

Your habits?

No, no, these other things, your consciousness, your intellect, your emotional structure, your stable state. If you don't buy that under ordinary conditions the only thing that survives about you is the accumulation of your habits, if you think something else survives beyond that, and you're willing to gamble on it, be my guest. If you're not willing to gamble on it, then you'd better start talking about the body of habits and accumulation of habits.

On one of your talks on habits you said that another name for the body of habits was essence.

In the Gurdjieffian sense, essence, and I also called it something else. Unconscious accumulation can be called karma, whereas the conscious creation of habits is called something quite different. And I also did not specify at that point what it is called.

At the time it didn't seem like I had enough relationship to my own habits. I came to the concrete understanding of habit, the massness of it, the mass of the habit — it survives everything — and what are its qualities, what could possibly survive everything, what kind of qualities would it have if I have this particular habit?

What habit are you talking about?

One habit is always starting on the spiritual path. I have the habit of starting.

Just starting?

Just starting, and I don't see... it's not the thought...

No, thoughts don't survive. One clue to that is that a habit does not have mass, and that's why it can survive. It has no mass, it has no specific location, it has no other qualities other than it is a habit. Another quality that it has is that it immediately imprints itself upon the nervous system the moment you enter a body. Not only that but you also have the drive to imprint that on other bodies, other nervous systems, and give it to other beings as habit. You have that drive also. But you're right, it's very hard to pin down why it survives. As we get into deeper work with the primal forms and the forms of the guides and the stages, particularly the second stage, the first part of the second stage, I think you'll begin to see why the habits continue, why they survive, why everything else about you does not.

You think of habits as something apart from yourself, then obviously you would survive. You think of you as an identity and your habits as something else other than your identity, something which complements your identity or which works along with your identity or in some ways shapes it. Then you misunderstand the nature of habits. But if you understand yourself as nothing but habits, the accumulation of habits plus a little spark of something or other, you understand that you cannot destroy habits, you cannot get rid of habits, you must substitute something else for a habit you do not wish to have. Then you understand that habits are an intrinsic part of your Being, that is why they survive.

E.J. Gold, *I'm Always Sitting At This Table,*
Pen and Ink, Rives BFK, 1987.

The Tank is Your Native State

Your Being functions through habit. It has no other way to function, and the Being may be seen as an intellect, if you wish, or as a conscious entity, although it neither is conscious nor an entity, nor does it have intellect, but it has the equivalent of a mind with which to guide itself through the created structure of existence and even through the tracklessness of non-existence (and uncreated or non-created or no longer created areas) and this thing which is equivalent to the mind is the body of habits. It's extremely simple, it has to be simple. It has to be streamlined in order to be a small enough package to survive. It only has 18 components, 9 positive and 9 negative, that's all it has. I mean polarity positive and polarity negative. I don't mean good and bad.

Right, well I was wondering polarity wise, would love and hate be an example?

Love and hate? No, those are not polarized habits.

That's 9 positive habits and 9 negative habits?

No it isn't. It's 18 major habit structures, each one of which could be composed of thousands or millions of habits. All of which comprise one single habitual structure. The body of habits is composed of 18 major functions, each one of which could have thousands or millions of minor functions or factors.

Would I have 18 different than him? Mine would be different than his?

Not as different as you might wish. The number of those combinations and individual habits might be quite large, but in terms of basic structure there can only be permutations of 18 single structures to its own factor. It actually runs out to about 10 to the minus 27th, on the low end and 10 to the 26th probably minus one on the top end, factorially, which means simply that that's a lot of habits, most of which are unimportant to change, deal with, fool with, or bother about.

Some of them you might consider extremely bad and yet they are extremely good for you in the work; others you might consider extremely good and yet they're bad for you in the work. What I was saying was that if you work on habits, if you wish that you had worked on habits yesterday, what can you do? If you hope to work on them tomorrow, what can you do? If you don't know what habits you're working with, what can you do? If you have no idea what you're doing, or where you are or what's occurring to you or what action you're taking in response to that, what can you do?

The only time you have the power to take an action is in present time. So, in a sense, if you wish to say that only now do you have any chance to make change, then yes, that's true. But just to observe now, isn't anywhere near enough.

You must act now, take the moment and act upon it, not just observe the moment. Observing the moment is by no means enough. Not only that, you must not only be able to act now and be willing to act in the present, but you also must know exactly how to act, what to do, specifically. There isn't a general rule for everyone, that's right for everyone. If there were it would have been put in a book, and everyone would have read the book, and followed it to the letter by now; but there is no such thing. Everyone has, because of the peculiarity of the psyche, a slightly different path to follow and slightly different work to do, although there are some general things that everyone can do. Especially in the very beginning there are a great many things that everyone can do, but eventually one must go on one's own in an individual way and still work with a group in a group way. Does that answer your question?

Yes, there was the point also that, the original question was about receiving grace from the guru, I don't know if that changes the question at all but it seems you have to be present to receive the teaching or higher initiation.

Not only must you be present but you must be present and ready for it. You have to be almost fully baked in order to receive the final cooking factor, and you must also be able to state exactly what it is that you want, and not want it with desire, and you also must at that point not be important. If what happens to you is important then you will utterly flub, completely fall apart at the reception of knowledge because you will try to maintain your identity, even though you may know completely within yourself that to maintain that identity is not good. Still at the last moment you may grasp for it. If you do, it'll be a long road coming back. It doesn't mean that you'd be utterly destroyed, it just means that it's a long road to haul back up the line again.

To be important is a habit, not only to worry for oneself and try to do, and try to arrange everything so that you are taken care of, you're secure, you're safe, everything is to your advantage, but even things like wondering what will become of you or worrying what will become of you, or choosing the right path for yourself, or the right thing for yourself, all of these things slow you down. Looking for just the right thing for you, working for your development, trying to decide what you should do next to best benefit yourself, these are all things which will slow you down, possibly trap you for a long time and maybe even worse. The point is that you must be able to let go of all those things, particularly let go of the concern for yourself.

Gurdjieff used to say, "Recognize your own nothingness," but he didn't mean that you aren't anything, that you're just a drop in the bucket or any of that. He meant that your nothingness is extremely important, to recognize your voidness if you wish, to recognize that for all practical purposes, you do not yet exist. YOU are not yet in existence. You have not yet created yourself. You are now just a bundle of accumulated habits. That's what your consciousness amounts to at this point and that is what your Beingness amounts to at this point. Just a bundle of accumulated habits. You might as well be a machine, even though you're not, because your habits are completely automatic, they will kick in under any stress whatsoever, and while you can be quite clever not under stress, when you are under stress you are your own Being. You are an essence at that time, and if your essence performs rather badly under stress then you understand that it needs some work; but more than that, you can see that your essence needs work when it goes against your wishes, when it goes

E.J.Gold, *Which Door?*,
Pen and Ink, Rives BFK, 1987.

against your decisions, when it goes against the things you decided would be best for yourself. Your essence needs work even when everything is going right for you. Now, what was your question?

Therefore, when you're talking about YOU and you're talking about essence and you're talking about habits, it's really those accumulated habits, right? I have the understanding that sometimes YOU refers to the Being.

Suppose it is. Of course, you are removed from or divorced from your habits, sometimes momentarily, sometimes you can see yourself as separate from your habits. However, under stress you are not divorced from your habits, and you are entirely unpredictable.

There are times when I experience myself as being a slave of a particular habit that I can see. You mentioned that you have to know how to replace a habit and I'd like to learn how to replace this specific habit that I can see.

Well, you're obviously talking about a habit having to do with relationships. I would rather that you first try to change a little habit. Instead of an elephant-sized habit like that one, it would perhaps be better for you to work on smaller ones. In any case, the habit that you described is not bad, what is harmful to you in the work and what is harmful to you in the attainment of conscious life is the fixation that you have on the object of your relationship.

That's the habit, is to make that fixation.

Oh, well that's not much of a habit at all.

Great, then it's a small habit.

No, it's not much of a habit in that it isn't a habit.

Ah, what is that?

That's something social. When you talk about a prime personal relationship, you're talking about something which is basically a cultural condition. Now, there is a habit behind that, behind all that, which is the absolute relationship that you have, the first relationship that you ever had with anything other than yourself, but that deals with the form of the guide. You tend to choose the form which is closest to that form, the ideal personal form of the guide that you tend to see and you chose all your relationships that way . That we can't touch for a while, but in terms of every day, I think we can very quickly put that to rest. Again, that habit is based upon your importance, that it's important to you what becomes of you, it's important whether you survive or don't survive, whether your influence in survival is extended or not, whether you leave a trail of yourself in the material universe. *Kilroy was here.* You leave your mark, you make some contribution and so on, and where are you really applying that? To the material universe? How long do you think that will last? You're going to outlast that by far, and yet you're trying desperately to survive through the material universe in some way.

The use of the word addiction is very good, and you could know about it and understand it and even know why you do it and yet have no power over it, in which case, we'll see you around here next time. Perhaps you can work up to it slowly. There are some things you could do about it. The problem is that those things all take time, and your time is extremely valuable, and I would think that you would rather use it to a better advantage. You have to be able to go somewhat above your addictions in order to remain in the work. You must have some kind of discipline, at least a little discipline. If we worked on all those things we'd very quickly run out of time because it takes a minimum of twenty years to make anything real occur. It has taken you trillions upon trillions of years to

E.J. Gold, *Are You In There?*,
Pen and Ink, Rives BFK, 1987.

make something occur that is not real, and we're only talking about twenty years against trillions and trillions of years.

Very few beings have it in them to make the decision to spend twenty years doing something consciously when they have spent trillions upon trillions of years doing something unconsciously, doing virtually the same thing. You will lose nothing by doing it. You have everything to gain, and yet you're going to be fighting yourself every minute to remain in the game. You know that everything you want you can have and that you probably will conceive of some other way of going about getting what you want and so take quite different actions and, as a result, get nothing like what you think you want. You could see this occur again and again. Someone will say, "Well, I really want this and the school can't give it to me, I can't get it at the school, I've got to go do such and such and that and that, and then I'll get such and such a thing." They go out and they do what they think will get them such and such and it turns out, maybe two weeks later, whatever it was they were after comes by here – had they remained they would have had it but instead they go off and don't get it. Well, of course, that should tell you right there that something very definite is occurring.

They are trying to keep what they want out there so they can continue to want it, because without that they would have no drive, they would have no purpose for their existence. Now a Being who has completed all of that, has gone through all of that stuff, has gone beyond it, a real Being's purpose for existence is existing, no more, no less. One exists to exist, one doesn't exist to do something or to have something or to be something else or to know something or to relate to something, one exists to exist. Whatever occurs within that structure is fine. So, you have a question?

I'd like to ask you, could you give an example of the 18 pairs of habits or large habit structures, an example of what that is?

Not right now. Right now I wanted to give you examples of tiny little habits, flea habits, that you can break, and as you get your biceps flexing, when you have a two-inch expansion, then we'll talk about that.

What kind of work can you do with your identity and self-importance?

It really is so wasteful to work on identity, self-importance, ego, because your time is much more valuable than that.

Yeah, I know, I don't mean work directly, I mean work... What could you do to lose self importance?

It's extremely simple. You could lose all of that if it' s important enough to you, simply by deciding to do that. It is a very simple decision.

And that would cancel out self-importance?

You could no longer manifest it. You could decide to no longer manifest it, decide to no longer run your life according to that. Some of the things that you could know for sure that are not good are your ideas of self-importance, your idea that what happens to you is important, what becomes of you is important, those are things that you definitely can do without.

Where you become afraid, you're becoming afraid for yourself. Where you become confused, what are you becoming confused about? Where you are, what you should do, what's happening to you. You can lose your continual round, endless round of considerations about what's happening to you, worries, fears, anxieties, complaints, by losing your desire to have something specific occur to you and to not have other specific things occur to you. There's a whole set must occur and this isn't okay to occur. Well, rather than handle every one of those things you simply turn to the source of it, and the source of that is, very simply, that you are an important Being. Really it is quite simple, you can know everything you need to know about this in about twenty minutes. The work on self is not complicated. It is extremely simple, but it takes about twenty years to apply it.

Does that have anything to do with loss of self -importance or death of the ego?

What do you mean?

Well, let's say you go through a death experience...

There are some things you could decide to do. There are other things that you cannot decide to do but must consciously go about making happen, and then there are other things that just happen by themselves provided you are on the path, provided you're working. One of the things that just happens by itself is ego death, identity death, it's something that you don't need to do. One of the things that does not happen by itself, that you must decide to do and the moment you decide to do it it does occur, is to release your self-importance, to agree that what occurs to you is not important, and that means that you understand the nature of your experiences. If you understand the nature of your experience, those things which occur to you are not important, those things which you do or don't do are not important, only what you are is important and right now you are not what you are, you are what you have become. There's a big difference. To be what you are you must create what you are, consciously . If you could do that as a matter of course without any help, then you would have done it long ago.

So, you need some knowledge about yourself before you could make that decision?

E.J.Gold, "What's Under The Rug?",
Pen And Ink, Rives BFK, 1987.

You must have complete self-knowledge, before you can work consciously on yourself. In other words, to be what you are rather than what you have become—but even while you are not what you are, you can decide to not be important. That can help you quite a bit. Can you imagine situations in which you realize your non-importance, in terms of what becomes of you, what happens to you? Your real importance is as a Being, not in terms of what you are doing as an activity. Your actions are not important, your Beingness is. Right now, your Beingness is becomingness, all automatic, unconscious accumulation. That isn't Beingness at all. There is no Beingness to it, no realness to it. If you are only unconscious accumulated habits and you are continuing to accumulate habits and you are continuing to be an accumulation of habits, you are not what you are becoming.

Why does it take twenty years to have something real happen?

I said at least twenty years. By the end of the first year when you work with this, you'll know whether it's working or not. That's why I ask you to make a commitment of one year, if you come in here seriously as a group. Now look, if you do something once, is it a habit?

No.

Okay, if you decide to make it a habit, is it a habit?

No.

If you have to constantly decide to do something, say that you constantly had to smoke a cigarette or decide to, say, touch your right ear, or you had to constantly decide to always start off walking with your left foot, every time you did it, is that a habit?

No.

So, only after a long period of repeated action does

something become a habit at all. It's not just a question of becoming automatic for a little while. You want it to become a habit for an extremely long time which means ruthlessly exterminating all the counter habits which could possibly (I'm going to use a word, I would like you to keep in mind that this word is chosen because there is no other available—but it's a word that can be easily misunderstood), you don't want associated habits with your major habits which could contaminate those habits over a long period of time. The contaminating habits would become worse and worse, larger and larger.

I'll give you an example of that: In space technology, if you make a correction, say you're going to do a moon shot, you make a correction of one degree, just as you're leaving the orbit around the earth, that one degree begins to grow and grow and grow relative to the moon. As you get closer and closer to the moon, it may be one degree from the earth but it's quite a bit more distance across. I can give you an idea of that with the blackboard. (He demonstrates with a drawing of a diverging line). Here is where we begin in this lifetime. You might begin with a habit, but you've got a contaminating habit. It's small, but by the time you reach this point that contaminating habit has taken you far off the mark. That's why you take twenty years. You take twenty years to insure that all of the contaminating factors have been thoroughly removed and that it is genuinely a habit with you and not something you have to think about. Now, that means also knowing how to make something a habit.... Realize that there are people in spiritual groups who have tried to make as a habit the spiritual life, and twenty years later they still have to think about it every time they do something. They still have to make a decision to do it.

Okay, so twenty years is minimal. It isn't something that you could be better at or worse at, there's just no way of being better at ingraining a habit than someone else, taking a short path, in that respect. That is a short path — twenty years is nothing. If you'd only realize that, even if you could just get the habit to come to a school, without having to depend upon your mind for that, without having to depend on your memory for that, without having to depend on your knowledge, on your personality, just as a habit, to make it to a school, if you did nothing but that in this lifetime, you would accomplish a very great deal for yourself.

What decision has to be made before you're willing to start in the work?

No, no, no, no, no, that all takes place as you go through all this stuff, when it's important enough to you without you being personally important, if that makes any sense to you. You must realize the importance of this, and you must realize the nature of what the world has to offer. There are other trips and you can get on them. There are trips of power, trips of knowledge, trips of understanding. There are all sorts of spiritual trips, all sorts of material trips, all kinds of emotional trips, all kinds of intellectual trips, all kinds of philosophical trips that you can go on, that you are free to go on; only when those things have nothing left to offer should you begin this work.

In the meantime, however, you can look at the work, think about it, sing about it, talk about it, but it's not wise to begin it until you have really, firmly committed yourself to it, because it's extremely painful to stop in the middle once you've begun. It creates even more suffering, until it's done. Imagine going to the dentist, having a toothache, and the dentist says, "Aha, there's a cavity right there," so he begins to drill and he's got the thing drilled and the cavity is all open and exposed and you suddenly jump up and run out of the office. That's a very foolish thing to do. You've made it worse, haven't you?

It's going to get worse, much worse. It would have been better to go through an entire procedure. There is an end to it. It isn't a forever thing. Well, it's the same thing with work on yourself, there is a definite end to the work. You do it only to a certain point, to completion point, and when it's finished it's finished. If you're in a hurry, it'll take longer. If you quit in the middle, it'll take much longer and be much more painful, and you'll have a lot more to deal with to fix it, but you see you took the first step in this a long time ago, or you wouldn't be here at this point. You wouldn't even be able to listen to this talk. You wouldn't be able to hear any of these ideas had you not taken the first step a long time ago.

So now the drilling has already begun some time ago, and you're in the middle of the drilling. It's uncomfortable, certainly it's uncomfortable, and you thought it would be over in maybe a couple of weeks, and you'd be enlightened and that would be the end of it. You looked at all the butterflies, and you thought, gosh they've made it and then you discovered that the butterflies aren't really butterflies, it's an imaginary trip that they're on. Just to hide the fact that they're on a real trip, they get onto some kind of other trip, and they imagine themselves to be butterflies, and they flit about in bliss, and they're just prolonging the agony, that really is what they are doing.

If they would only move through it, it would take a very short time and it would be over with. So much unnecessary suffering is caused by imagination. Remember, I was talking this afternoon about imagination, I've talked about

E.J.Gold, *Keep The Beat*,
Pen and Ink, Rives BFK, 1987.

this before relative to the tank but I'll mention it again.

When you get in the tank you basically are getting into your native state. You get into the tank, you lie down for a while and then you get back up and you leave the tank and that's where your trip begins. Now, if you want to trip out in the tank, that's up to you but really, that's imagination. That's a totally imaginary thing that's occurring with you. The trip begins when you leave the tank. The trip ends when you enter the tank, it's as simple as that. The same thing is true with transit: the trip doesn't begin at the point of death and end at rebirth. The trip begins at rebirth and ends at death. That's the trip, the rest is reality, just as it is in its simplest, most straightforward form or non-form.

Are you saying that any phenomenon that happens in the tank is imaginary?

Yes, if you want to find out what composes your mind and what your mind is made of and how well you could project images and how well you could put yourself into imaginary spaces, then that's an excellent tool. It's a wonderful tool for exploring the psyche, the mind, the body, the nervous system, and the projective ability of the mind to conquer boredom. That is the goal. No one wants to just lie down in the tank. Boring! So, you start showing movies. Everybody knows they've got a 16 mm projector behind each eyeball and two to run it, so you start showing home movies as soon as you get in the tank. And now, here's our summer vacation, and in this slide, and here I am doing a . . ., and here we are with a . . . That's the slide show and then we have the Super 8 stuff, and the 16 mm stuff.

Oh, oh, I forgot, here are the porno films over here, here are your spiritual films right here, here's one where I went to Alturas, look at that, I never thought I'd get out of that one — and the film rolls on and on and on and you have gained nothing, you have changed nothing, you've done nothing other than look at some home movies. You could subtitle every one of those home movies:

How I Influenced Myself Through No Fault of My Own, or,
Me Myself and I,
Some of Me,
Beyond Me,
Return of Me,
Sort of Me,
Life of Me,
Me and I Meet Myself,
The Were-Me, The King of Me, The Egg of Me,
The Planet of Me,
A Me For All Seasons,
O Lucky Me — that's good —
The Longest Me,
My Fair Me — that's good —
On a Clear Me,
Two Thousand and Me Odyssey,
Little Big Me,
Me Goes to the Beach, Me Goes to the Races,
The Road to Me,
Me Soup,
The Greatest Me Ever Told — that's good —
Gone With Me — yeah, big box office —
Meport, Meport 75,
Clockwork Me.

Anyway you see how it can get out of hand.

If you could really get into the non-importance of what becomes of you, if you could translate that for others in their own terms or if you could transmit it to others in a way that they would understand it for themselves, they would just come to the school and that would be the end of that, no questions. All these questions are reflections of your worry of what will become of you: whether you're in good hands or not, whether I'm responsible toward you, whether I know enough to be sure to give you what you need, to make sure that it's going to be okay for you. If you could simply learn to live without that worry you would do much better. Don't worry about whether I know anything or not, don't worry about whether I'm able to deliver the teaching to you or not, don't worry whether there is a teaching or not, don't worry about whether there's something that could be done about anything, don't worry about whether or not there's anything that needs to be done. Maybe there isn't, maybe this is just a whole useless trip, totally useless, this is a total waste of your life (only someone who has a precious life could possibly waste it).

But on the other hand, if you don't have the idea that you don't have much time to do something, how do you keep those two things together?

I don't know that any balance can be obtained between those two things. Don't worry about it, it may totally screw you up. What's the worst thing that could possibly happen to you? You come into this school and what's the worst that could happen to you? You waste twenty years? What could you do with your life that is so important? See, in any case your life is worthless. You might as well just throw it into the work because it's useless by itself. Not only that, but your life will not survive anything, what you do in this life will not survive.

A lot of people will throw away survival for imaginary

survival; will throw away virtually, what amounts to immortality, (beyond immortality, because it even survives existence itself), in exchange for a few crummy years of suffering, of imaginary pleasure, after which they'll be reduced to their automatic habits.

See what nonsense that is?

Any other questions?

About The Author

John Lilly

John C. Lilly, M.D., an unparalleled scientific visionary and explorer, has made significant contributions to psychology, brain research, computer theory, medicine, ethics, and interspecies communication. His work launched the global interest in dolphins and whales, provided the basis for the movie *Day of the Dolphin,* and stimulated the enactment of the Marine Mammal Protection Act. Lilly's interest in the nature of human consciousness led him to invent the isolation tank in the 1950's. In the early sixties, Lilly encountered LSD and soon took his experiments with this mind changer to the isolation tank. The hair-raising experiences that resulted formed the essence of the movie *Altered States.*

Lilly's life and work at the forefronts of human knowledge encompass the major themes of the twentieth century. His dozen books have sold millions of copies worldwide. A distinguished brain researcher even before he became a public figure, Lilly has sown the seeds of several scientific revolutions, including the theory of internal realities, the hardware/software model of the human brain/mind, and the initiation of worldwide efforts at interspecies communications with large-brained cetaceans.

Devoted to a philosophical quest for the nature of reality, Lilly pursued a brilliant academic career among the scientific leaders of the day, mastering one science after another and eventually achieving a perspective that transcends the centuries-old conflict between rationality and mysticism. He has lived in the company of associates and intimates including Nobel physicists Richard Feynman and Robert Milliken, philosophers Buckminster Fuller, Aldous Huxley, and Alan Watts, psychotherapy pioneers R.D. Laing and Fritz Perls, spiritual teachers Oscar Ichazo and Baba Ram Dass, and a host of luminaries–inventors, writers, and Hollywood celebrities.

Today, at the age of 80, John Lilly stands as the twentieth century's foremost scientific pioneer of the inner and outer limits of human experience. He is a relentless adventurer whose "search for Reality" has led him repeatedly to risk life and limb, but whose quests have resulted in astonishing insights into what it means to be a human being in an ever more mysterious universe.

–from *John Lilly So Far*

We all saw John C. Lilly as some sort of wizard, a science-fiction starman, a unique back-to-the-future alchemist. A new Paracelsus. A veritable Isaac Newton of the Mind. I am convinced that there has never been anyone quite like J.C. Lilly. He can be understood best in the terms of quantum physics. J.C. is a singularity. A prime number, divided only by himself and One. —Timothy Leary, foreword to *The Scientist*

About the Author

E.J. Gold

    E.J. Gold has been a prominent and controversial figure in the Human Potential movement in California for over 25 years. Technically a " shamanic Rabbi," he earned respect in the field of transformational psychology by the clarity, profundity, uniqueness, and expertise of his writings and thoughts. His early publications in the mid to late sixties in the area of transformational psychology and spiritual growth already emphasized a practical approach toward inner awakening and transformation.

    Thus far he has written over two dozen books in the field. The subjects he covers range from attention and presence, the waking state, death and dying, to practical work on self, shamanism, labyrinth voyaging, shape-shifting, Bardotown (the City of the Dead), artifact reading, imprinting and use, cosmic laws, the suffering of the Absolute, higher bodies, hidden work, artistic mystical visions and expressions, the Tarot, prayers, sacrifice, sufism, shakti, natural childbirth, and many more themes. After 20 years of circulation by Gateways Book Gold's *The American Book of the Dead* has been published in1995 by Harper San Francisco.

    Gold's network in transformational psychology is extensive. He has worked with groups, fine-tuning his language and method in workshops at Cowichan Center, East-West House, Odiyan, East-West Foundation, and many other centers of spiritual activity throughout North America in the 70's. He has been described as a teacher's teacher.

His influence and association with contemporaries includes Robert S. de Ropp, Reshad Feild, Fritz Perls, Claudio Naranjo, John Lilly, Timothy Leary, Robert Anton Wilson, Swami Vishnu Devananda, Tarthang Tulku Rinpoche, Paul Anderson, Rick Edelstein (L.A. Movement editor), Guru Raj Singh, Amanda Foulger (a co-organizer of the 1978 International World Symposium), Dr. Bronner, The Flying Karamazov Brothers, Joan Halifax, Samuel Avital, Antonio Asin, Heather Valencia, and many more.

In spite of all these associations and his remarkable lists of accomplishments, Gold has maintained a high level of privacy and isolation from the media, which he cherishes. He has never been highly marketed and will never be " just another stop" on the guru superhighway.

Gold attributes some of his versatility and universality as a transformational psychologist and consciousness explorer to his culturally-privileged background. As the son of H.L. Gold, the famous founding editor of Galaxy Science Fiction Magazine, he grew up surrounded by such luminaries as Frank Herbert, Isaac Asimov, Harlan Ellison, Theodore Sturgeon, Robert Silverberg, Alfred Bester, Robert Heinlein, Arthur C. Clarke, to name a few. Other celebrities associated with his family included geniuses from the arts and the sciences—John Cage, Merce Cunningham, Sir Julian Huxley, Ben Shahn, Oscar Levant, Charles Laughton and Elsa Manchester.

Gold is internationally known as an originator of contemporary processes of transformational psychology and a masterful proponent of proven ancient methods of labyrinth voyaging. He is a leader in the field of consciousness.

Dear Reader of *Tanks for the Memories,*

This book is a manual for your use, self-contained and self-explanatory.

It can also be a gateway, the threshold to a great inner adventure. If you are one of those readers who not only reads the exercises but also applies them to gather your own experimental results—you may be ready for more tools to further your explorations and experiments.

For a current catalog and referral to related books and study materials, you may contact Gateways at the address below with no obligation to purchase.

Gateways Books and Tapes
P.O. Box 370-TM
Nevada City, CA 95959
(800) 869-0658 or (530) 271-2239
www.gatewaysbooksandtapes.com
email: info@gatewaysbooksandtapes.com

A Partial List of Titles You Can Order
(See www.gatewaysbooksandtapes.com for complete book list)

by E.J. Gold
American Book of the Dead
The Great Adventure: Talks on Death, Dying and the Bardos
The Human Biological Machine as a Transformational Apparatus
Parallel Worlds Explored
Practical Work on Self
The Hidden Work
The Seven Bodies of Man
Visions in the Stone (Intro. by Robert Anton Wilson)

by Michael Hutchison
The Book of Floating: Exploring the Private Sea

by John C. Lilly, M.D.
The Deep Self
The Mind of the Dolphin: A Nonhuman Intelligence

For more information about floating and places to float:
www.floatation.com
www.FloatationLocations.com